Owning the Secular

Owning the Secular examines three case studies dealing with religious symbols and cultural identity, including two public controversies over the veil in Canada – at the federal level and in the province of Québec – and an ex-Muslim podcaster rethinking her atheist identity in the era of Donald Trump and the alt-right.

Drawing on theories of discourse analysis and ideology critique, this study calls attention to an evolution in how secularism, nationalism, and multiculturalism in Euro-Western states are debated and understood as competing groups contest and rearrange the meaning of these terms. This is especially true in the digital age as online cultures have transformed how information is spread, how we imagine our communities, build alliances, and produce shared meaning.

From recent attempts to prohibit religious symbols in public, to Trump's so-called Muslim bans, to growing disenchantment with the promises of digital media, this study turns the lens how nation-states, organizations, and individuals attempt to "own" the secular to manage cultural differences, shore up group identity, and stake a claim to some version of Western values amidst the growing uncertainties of neoliberal capitalism.

Matt Sheedy is Visiting Assistant Professor in North American Studies at the University of Bonn, Germany.

In this intellectual *étude*, Sheedy takes us to the very heart of secularism's – and by extension, the West's – fragility. Discourses of values, he deftly shows, are neither ontological nor natural, but often political slogans awaiting convenient manipulation when needed. The result is a timely, well-informed, and nuanced analysis that deserves wide attention.

Aaron W. Hughes, *University of Rochester, USA*

While scholars of religion once saw their objects of study as unique and set apart, those acquiring the tools of social theory find that their research has far wider application, helping us to understand how groups and identities work. Matt Sheedy represents this second camp, offering a timely analysis of how our secular world functions: its beneficiaries and its challenges, as well as its possibilities. *Owning the Secular* nicely exemplifies why those who don't usually read scholars of religion would be well served to change that habit, for religion is never really about religion but, instead, about how we organize ourselves, how we authorize our worlds, and how we marshal the forces to contest the worlds of others.

Russell T. McCutcheon, *University of Alabama, USA*

Owning the Secular is a superb study of the theory, culture, and politics of all facets of secularity in the twenty-first century. It's particularly valuable for the way it links the political and intellectual coordinates of the secular to its most dynamic contemporary ecosystem: the whirlpool of 24-hour news media, podcasts, clips, pop-up protests, and social media posts. Matt Sheedy has creatively arranged a broad range of sources into a convincing argument about the digital secular.

Donovan Schaefer, *University of Pennsylvania, USA*

Routledge Focus on Religion

Visual Thought in Russian Religious Philosophy
Pavel Florensky's Theory of the Icon
Clemena Antonova

American Babylon
Christianity and Democracy Before and After Trump
Philip S. Gorski

Avantgarde Art and Radical Material Theology
A Manifesto
Petra Carlsson Redell

Pandemic, Ecology and Theology
Perspectives on COVID-19
Edited by Alexander J. B. Hampton

Trump and History
Protestant Reactions to 'Make America Great Again'
Matthew Rowley

Theology and Climate Change
Paul Tyson

Religion and Euroscepticism in Brexit Britain
Ekaterina Kolpinskaya and Stuart Fox

Owning the Secular
Religious Symbols, Culture Wars, Western Fragility
Matt Sheedy

For more information about this series, please visit: www.routledge.com/Routledge-Focus-on-Religion/book-series/RFR

Owning the Secular

Religious Symbols, Culture Wars, Western Fragility

Matt Sheedy

LONDON AND NEW YORK

First published 2022
by Routledge
2 Park Square, Milton Park, Abingdon, Oxon OX14 4RN

and by Routledge
605 Third Avenue, New York, NY 10158

Routledge is an imprint of the Taylor & Francis Group, an informa business

British Library Cataloguing-in-Publication Data
A catalogue record for this book is available from the British Library

Library of Congress Cataloging-in-Publication Data
A catalog record has been requested for this book

ISBN: 978-0-367-46802-6 (hbk)
ISBN: 978-1-032-08016-1 (pbk)
ISBN: 978-1-003-03123-9 (ebk)

DOI: 10.4324/9781003031239

Typeset in Times New Roman
by Apex CoVantage, LLC

For Leader (Mom)

Contents

Acknowledgments

I would like to thank Rebecca Shillabeer, my editor at Routledge, for proposing this volume to me after reading a blog post that I wrote in 2019 on Québec's latest religious symbols ban. I would also like to thank Amy Doffegnies at Routledge for her patience and support. Much thanks goes to Rory Dickson for his helpful suggestions for chapter 1. I am also grateful to the folks involved with the American Examples 2020 Fellowship at the University of Alabama, in Tuscaloosa, where I workshopped a first draft of chapter 3. Likewise, I am grateful to the master's students in my North American Atheisms class at the University of Bonn (Vanessa Baldyga, Daria Kolometcevia, Rafael Mukhametdinov, Luis Ontiveros-Meza, Anne Niesen, Sara Salar, Jennifer Schmitz, and Insiah Zaidi) for offering helpful comments on a draft of chapter 3.

Introduction

Translating the secular

Writing shortly after September 11, 2001, German philosopher Jürgen Habermas revisits the question of secularization in light of the terrorist attacks on US soil. Near the end of his essay, Habermas proposes the following idea for Western countries to consider:

> The mode for nondestructive secularization is translation. This is what the Western world, as the worldwide secularizing force, may learn from its own history. If it presents this complex image of itself to other cultures in a credible way, intercultural relations may find a language other than that of the military and the market alone.
>
> (2003: 114)

When Habermas talks of the West's own history, he is referring to the period of time following the Protestant Reformation (c. 1517), which saw the gradual transition away from theocratic rule in many European kingdoms toward something resembling the kind of 'secular' nation-states that we recognize today. Habermas suggests that the West would do well to consider how its own history of bloody conflict was partly resolved by the adoption of secular norms, which he understands to be the cornerstone of liberal, democratic societies. He also claims that it was only by translating competing religious doctrines into a shared secular language that Euro-Western states were able to create conditions that opened up space for cooperation. This includes certain rules or procedures of interaction, where all must come to accept the "internal logic of secular knowledge" and must grant "priority to secular reasons" in the political arena (2008: 137).

Anthropologist Talal Asad takes up this problem of translation in his most recent book *Secular Translations* (2018), noting that while it is important to try to understand "the native's point of view," "it is quite another [thing] for the anthropologist to approach 'the native' with the possibility of learning something important for her own form of life that might help to transform how that life is understood" (9). What Asad is ultimately asking us to consider here is whether "secular knowledge" and "secular reasons" actually reflect a neutral ground for 'mutual perspective taking' as Habermas would put it? Unlike many examinations of this topic, I am less interested in offering prescriptions for how we might solve these problems, however much they may be implicit in some of my arguments. Instead, my goal is to demonstrate the fluid nature of the secular as a category of state power, shared principles, and identity.

Throughout this book, I use the phrase 'owning the secular' to point to two related ideas. In the first sense, 'own' refers to the use of a concept that makes claim to a certain tradition of practice in a clear and definable way. This can be done by referring to specific principles or values, as when deciding what laws are considered legitimate for adjudicating the claims of competing groups. Many people will own secular values such as individual freedom when defending their right to hold certain beliefs or engage in certain practices. Others will own the secular in more strategic ways that rely on the ambiguity of this term and its various applications. In this latter sense, the secular is not so much a clear set of guidelines for social behavior as it is a tool of persuasion, where its meaning depends upon the ability of people to use it in ways that are convincing to others.

The second way that I refer to 'owning' is one that has become popular in online cultures. As the Cambridge English dictionary defines it: "to defeat someone completely or be much better than him or her; to perform extremely well" (Cambridge 2021). Similar to the strategic use of the secular noted in the first example, this sense of owning points to a style of interaction and behavior that has been amplified through social media. As I will discuss in chapters 1 and 3, social media platforms have increasingly created algorithms that cater to people's ideological preferences, and incentivized modes of interaction that encourage defeating one's imagined opponent over engaging critically with ideas. The enticement to own someone complicates ideals of fairness and 'pubic reason' in ways that scholars of digital media have likened to online 'trolling.'

As Jon Ronson observes in his book *So You've Been Publicly Shamed*, trolls play on human vulnerabilities and are particularly adept at knowing what will trigger them. Following the election of Donald Trump, many have argued that trolling went mainstream as Trump normalized this mode of political communication through his Twitter feed. In this sense, owning reflects how new media has amplified polarization, and made it more difficult to claim any shared ground of principles, values, or meaning. From this perspective, it's culture wars all the way down. Although culture wars have always existed (if only by another name), dividing people on the basis of their habits and preferences, social media has developed new ways to weaponize these vulnerabilities that reflect hitherto unprecedent challenges for navigating the conflicts and clashes that the secular has, at its best, aimed to manage and keep at bay. With this virtual terrain in mind, I aim to map some contemporary currents of the digital secular.

In chapter 1, I lay out some secular territories by considering the secular and related concepts as they have developed in scholarship since the 1960s. Here I pay particular attention to how scholars began to reconsider these concepts starting in the 1990s and discuss how newer concepts like 'post-secularism' have complicated these ideas in ways that reflect what I am calling Western fragility. In part two of this chapter, I look at culture wars in the United States as a counter-force or 'id' (to use Freudian language) that complicates the idea of Western secular reason.

Chapter 2 turns to veiling controversies in Euro-Western nation-states and includes an overview of common tropes about Muslim women since the eighteenth century, as well as recent legal rulings on the veil in Europe. Next, I turn to two case studies in Canada. The first involves what became known as the niqab affair, where during the 2015 federal election one women's court challenge against a little-known restriction on the niqab rose to the level of a full-blown culture war that dominated Canadian media for the better part of a year. The second case looks at the province of Québec, and how numerous attempts to restrict niqabs led to a ban on all religious symbols from the public service.

In chapter 3, I pose the question, "are ex-Muslims atheists"? Whereas chapters 1 and 2 are mainly concerned with how the secular functions in the political realm and how it works as a form of national and (Western) civilizational identification, in this final chapter, I explore how self-proclaimed secularists have tied these labels to popular atheism as it developed in the post-9/11 period. Here I consider how ex-Muslims have aligned with so-called New Atheist ideas and examine the changing views of one ex-Muslim atheist podcaster, Eiynah, whose growing discomfort with these terms highlights the fluidity and fragility of secular identity.

Works cited

Asad, T. 2018. *Secular Translations: Nation-State, Modern Self, and Calculative Reason*. New York: Columbia University Press.

Habermas, J. 2003. Faith and Knowledge. In: H. Beister, W. Rehg, trans., *The Future of Human Nature*. Cambridge, UK: Polity Press, pp. 101–115.

Habermas, J. 2008. Religion in the Public Sphere: Cognitive Presuppositions for the "Public Use of Reason" by Religious and Secular Citizens. In: C. Cronin, trans., *Between Naturalism and Religion*. Cambridge, UK: Polity Press, pp. 114–148.

Cambridge. 2021. "Owning." Cambridge Dictionary Online. Available at: https://dictionary.cambridge.org/dictionary/english/owning [Accessed 20 January 2021].

1 The secular and the culture wars

Mapping some secular territories

Studies of 'the secular,' which I use throughout this book as an umbrella term to describe a cluster of related concepts such as secularization, secularism, and secularity, have grown exponentially in the twenty-first century. Following the collapse of the Soviet Union in the early 1990s and its various forms of state-imposed secularism, the role of religion in global affairs became a topic of growing interest among pundits and scholars alike. After the 9/11 attacks, this interest grew to a near obsession, as fears of political Islam dominated public discourse for over a decade, and were reactivated with each and every terrorist attack on Western soil. The fall of the Soviet Union also deprived the West of one of its most potent scapegoats, 'godless communism,' creating space for a variety of atheist and nonreligious identities to expand like never before. These and other factors have contributed to a serious rethinking of the secular, what it means, and how it works as a form of power to inform our sense of shared identity and shared values.

My own approach to the secular takes this question of power seriously, which means paying attention to how organizations, governments, media, and scholars alike make use of this concept for particular ends. By focusing on how the secular is used by competing social actors, I aim to call attention to the importance of contextualizing and historicizing these concepts rather than assume some stable meaning. Brent Nongbri provides one of many examples of this problem on the distinction between religion and the secular during the Middle Ages when he writes, "In late medieval Latin (and even in English), these words described different kinds of Christian clergy, with *religiosus* describing members of monastic orders and *saecularis* describing Christian clergy not in a monastic order" (2013: 5). In this instance, religious and secular refer to different types of ecclesiastical roles within Catholic monastic communities and not to a distinction between church and state as it is commonly thought of today.[1]

DOI: 10.4324/9781003031239-1

Skipping ahead a few centuries, the famed French *Encyclopédie* connects the secular to the Peace of Westphalia of 1648, when German princes "seized the property of bishops, abbés and monks that were situated on their estates" (qtd. in Scott 2018: 11). This treatise, which ended the so-called wars of religion in parts of Europe (Cavanaugh 2009),[2] helped to establish the principle of *state sovereignty* by granting (Christian) rulers the right to decide which religion(s) would be practiced in their territories. This transfer of power from Rome to various 'Christian states' highlights the strong historical connection between state secularism and Christianity (to be discussed in chapter 2), including a preference for certain types of national religious authority, as seen with Church of England, as well as a rejection of ecclesiastical power, as seen in France. On the latter point, Joan Scott observes, "[b]y the time of the French Revolution, the secular referred to the state and its representatives in opposition to the church and the clergy" (2018: 11), thus marking a shift that would inform contemporary uses of the French term 'laïcité.'[3]

The generally accepted starting point for modern studies of *secularization* is Max Weber's work in sociology. Even here, however, we enter into a chicken-and-egg problem as to what came before his influential work, and whether the paradigm shifts that we attribute to thinkers like Weber today might be thought about differently if we move the timeline back further, drawing on other theorists, writers, artists, cultural traditions, political systems, and so forth. For example, to this list, we could also add August Comte, Karl Marx, Emile Durkheim, and Sigmund Freud, among many others, all of whom maintained that religion would gradually fade as industrialization spread across the globe.

Throughout the twentieth century, the term *secularization* was often used to reflect a teleological view of progress by marking a clear line of social development or evolution from primitive to modern societies. In many cases, these models have been used as empirical evidence to make claims about the superiority of certain religions, cultures, or civilizations over others (Masuzawa 2005; Arnal & McCutcheon 2015).[4] While most older classifications of the secular don't quite fit contemporary political orders, the idea of the secular as a form of progress or enlightenment continues to have some resonance as a way to distinguish the (Christian) 'West' from 'Islam,' especially in the post-9/11 period.

One seemingly benign example of this tendency can be found in Andrew Copson's *Secularism: A Very Short Introduction* (2019), where he writes that a "seed of a distinction" between church and state can be seen in the work of ancient writers such as Augustine (354–430), with his famous division between the 'City of God' and the 'City of Man' (8–9). While it is true that Augustine's work has been influential in discourses on the secular, by placing it on a continuum of 'Western' thought that includes ancient Greek and Roman thinkers as the foundation for modern forms of secularism, Copson (unintentionally?) politicizes this historical influence as a "seed" connecting Christianity to modern liberal democracy. As I will discuss later, this lineage is selective at best and ultimately functions to naturalize a Euro-Christian view of history.

Another common distinction worth noting is between secularism as a *worldview* and secularism as a *political project*. As Joseph Blankholm points out, George Holyoake, who coined the term 'secularism' in 1851, viewed it as a philosophy and way of life that influenced a variety of social movements going by this name. "By the late nineteenth century," Blankholm writes, "political secularism was synonymous with the separation of church and state, and philosophical secularism meant the beliefs of nonbelievers and their focus on living ethically in the physical world" (2020: 28).[5] The conflation of these two distinct categories has sometimes led to a rejection of political secularism on the grounds that it is anti-religious (e.g., in parts of the United States or Iran). Alternately, aspects of worldview secularism can inform the political identity of states, as seen in contemporary France and Québec, where one's ability to properly embody secularism (however, defined) becomes a key marker of citizenship and national belonging.

While the secular is often used to describe the type of power that religious authorities hold within states, it is less clear how *worldview secularism* functions as a form of identity. For example, Baker and Smith (2015) describe 'secularity' in terms of three categories: non-affiliated believers, people who actively reject theism, and those who remain agnostic on questions relating to the supernatural (16). In this sense, secularity points to those who do not have any significant affiliation with a religious institution, regardless of their beliefs. For political theorist William E. Connolly, however, to be a secularist is to support a political ideology that adheres to Western forms of reason.[6] While both of these descriptions may be useful for identifying certain types of beliefs and practices and, in Connolly's case, for uncovering a common ideology that informs the political use of this term, in neither case do they address how individuals who are lumped into these categories might define *themselves*.

Perhaps one reason for this is that people don't commonly identify as secular before, say, describing themselves as liberal or conservative, Democratic or Republican, Muslim, feminist, Christian, atheist, libertarian, and so forth. Identifying as secular is more likely to come about in the course of discussing political or cultural preferences and not through everyday exchanges. As I will discuss in chapter 3, self-described secular organizations have been common for well over a century. While these organizations reflect variations of worldview secularism, they also reflect strategic acts of differentiation, where the use of 'secular' (as in Secular Coalition for America) may signal a desire to be more inclusive of various groups, or to avoid the stigma attached to the term 'atheist.'

If secularity is best described as a type of disposition, then it can only come about through the cultivation of certain habits and practices over time, and through finding affinity with social groups that self-identify in this way. For example, identifying as secular may include a desire to assert certain positive rights, such as freedom of expression and speech. This particular use of the secular has motivated many who reject the influence of organized religion, including many ex-Muslims who have gravitated toward secular ideas and organizations as a way to legitimize their rejection of Islam (see chapter 3). However, since the secular might also include self-identifying religious practitioners, atheists, and, increasingly, defenders of a Western-centric worldview (regardless of religious identity), the stability of this term as a marker of identity remains elusive, to say the least.

Secularization reconsidered

In his 1996 essay, "Secularism in Retreat," acclaimed Austrian-American sociologist of religion Peter Berger declared that the once-popular secularization theory that he had so forcefully defended was "essentially mistaken" (3). According to Berger, "The key idea of secularization theory is simple and can be traced to the Enlightenment: Modernization necessarily leads to a decline of religion, both in society and in the minds of individuals" (4).[7] In his revised thesis, Berger noted that "experiments with secularized religion have generally failed," that "new religious beliefs and practices have nevertheless continued in the lives of individuals," and that "reactionary supernaturalism" of the Islamic and Evangelical varieties was on the rise. The only exception to this rule was Western Europe, where there had been a steady decline in "expressed beliefs," church attendance, along with traditional views on sexuality, social mores, etc. (8).

Although Berger's reconsideration was a useful intervention that helped to spur a new round of debate on this topic, his revised model continued to fashion secularization as a historical process whose time had not yet come. Despite adjustments to his theory, he remained enmeshed in Euro-Western assumptions about the means and ends of historical progress, especially when it comes to the fate of non-Western cultures. For example, Berger notes that while the "Evangelical upsurge" began in the United States, its spread to other parts of the world has become thoroughly "indigenous" in regions such as Latin America. While this is not a controversial claim in itself, Berger's framing of the problem is suggestive of deeper ideological assumptions, as when he writes:

> [A]n argument can be made that the Islamic resurgence has a strong tendency toward a negative view of modernity; in places it's downright anti-modern or counter-modernizing (as in its view on the role of women). By contrast the Evangelical resurgence is positively modernizing in most places it occurs, clearly so in Latin America.
>
> (1996: 10)

There are two points that I want to flag here that will bear on my arguments in later chapters. The first is that Berger makes no mention of the various colonial and imperial interests that have been tied to this "evangelical resurgence." As Melani McAlister (2018) demonstrates, the spread of American evangelicalism around the world in the postwar period was intimately tied to the politics of the Cold War, especially to military and foreign policy efforts in the Middle East and Africa. More specifically, McAlister shows how lobbying for humanitarian aid was often tied to evangelical missionizing efforts, along with human rights initiatives, including the promotion of 'religious freedom' around the world.

In her book dealing with the impacts of Euro-Western religious freedom projects, Elizabeth Shakman Hurd (2015) observes how "these efforts led to a politics defined by religious *difference* [my emphasis], privilege forms of religion favored by those who write laws, control resources, and govern societies, and marginalize other modes of belief, being, and belonging" (xi). With these considerations in mind, we might say that Berger's rosy picture of a "modernizing" evangelicalism fails to account for how political interests have enabled certain types of religious identification to *appear* modern by virtue of their connection to geopolitical power. Considering the alliance between many evangelical organizations in the United States with Donald Trump, it is hard to imagine that scholars would support this thesis today (see Brittain 2018).

The second point to flag is that Berger constructs Islam as a primary and stable identity that acts as *the* driving force behind "anti-modern" politics. As I will argue throughout this book, religion is best understood as a contested concept that is shaped by a variety of political, cultural, and economic variables that enable certain modes of religious identification to prevail over others.

Following Shakman Hurd, and contrary to Berger's claims, I argue that trying to determine which religion has proven itself to be more modern is a thoroughly political act that does not stand up to critical analysis. Indeed, such claims only make sense when deploying a narrow and self-serving definition of religion (typically of the liberal, 'enlightened' variety) as though it could be measured on a scale from primitive to modern. By contrast, when we foreground the politics behind constructions of religion and the secular, we place ourselves in a better position to analyze these concepts as contested categories that are constantly being gerrymandered to fit with particular identities and interests.

From secularization to secularisms

One of the more influential studies that contributed to a change in how scholars view secularization is José Casanova's *Public Religions in the Modern World* (1994). In his book, Casanova dates the "deprivatization" of religion back to the Iranian Revolution in 1979, followed by several other Christian-led political movements throughout the 1980s in Spain, Poland, Brazil, and the United States. Contrary to popular theories of secularization in the 1960s and 1970s that viewed new religious movements, religious experimentation, and new religious consciousness as the wave of the future (Bellah 2006b), Casanova argues that the 1980s saw a "repoliticization of the private religious and moral spheres" (4–5) as Catholic-led movements rejected authoritarian rule in countries such as Spain, Poland, and Brazil by promoting a pluralist civil society. For Casanova, these events not only called into question the idea that religious affiliation in the Euro-West was in decline, but also challenged the perception that expressions of religion ought to be kept private in order for a pluralistic civil society to thrive – a view that we'll see expand with theories of post-secularism starting in the late 1990s.

Casanova was not the first to challenge some of the major tenants of secularization theory. The American sociologist Talcott Parsons, for example, argued that differentiation (e.g., the structural separation of the Church from state, scientific, and legal authority) in the United States did not lead to a decline in confessional organizations but was rather an enabling factor that helped religion to find its 'proper' role – namely, as voluntary associations that could function in tandem with what Robert Bellah called American "civil religion." While leading sociologists of religion such as Peter Berger, Thomas Luckmann, Bryan Wilson, and Karel Dobbelaere all contributed to the idea that religion was inevitably in decline, others, such as David Martin and Andrew Greenly, were among the first to suggest that there was little evidence for this thesis.[8]

During the 1980s, Rodney Stark and William Sims Bainbridge also challenged the idea of progressive secularization by arguing that the persistent renewal of religion was a product of competition, which later influenced economic theories of religion linked to rational choice theory (Iannaccone 2010).[9] Elements of Stark and Bainbridge's theories can also be seen in the influential work of Pippa Norris and Ronald Inglehart (2004), whose book *Sacred and*

Secular drew on twenty years of data from the World Values Survey and concluded that the main tenants of secularization theory still hold true. The crux of their theory is that religious affiliation directly correlates with how much "existential security" people have in their lives. Higher levels of existential security are associated with strong welfare states (e.g., much of Western Europe), while lower levels of social security (e.g., the United States) are linked with higher rates of religious affiliation.

Commenting on the state of this scholarship, Gorski and Altinordu (2008) argue that the circular logic and (often) self-fulfilling nature of these theories create an impasse where "secularization theory becomes a vehicle for a secularist politics in which religion is aligned with tradition, superstition, and supernaturalism and kindred categories, whereas secularity is aligned with modernity, rationality, and science" (61). As a corrective to these approaches, Gorski and Altinordu offer two strategies, which I take up throughout this book. The first strategy is to foreground the politics of the secular and make sure that one's use of it is as analytically precise as possible. For example, they suggest that "when analyzing the historically Christian countries, one could substitute unchurching or de-Christianization for individual-level secularization without any loss in meaning," thus avoiding broad generalizations "about the nature and future of religion *tout court*" (75). Second, they suggest treating secularization through stipulative or "ideal-typical" definitions instead of assuming that it carries a self-evident meaning. In other words, they suggest 'owning' the secular. While I appreciate the latter suggestion, I will mostly be relying on the former strategy of using precise terms in an effort to uncover how the secular is being used for particular purposes.

Secularisms

The work of Talal Asad is one of the first examples of a turn in scholarship toward challenging the idea that religion and the secular are distinct and separate categories. For Asad, one of the most overlooked aspects of the secular is how it functions as a form of governance by providing a veneer of legitimacy to laws, institutions, and social norms under the presumption that it is neutral. Much like Michel Foucault demonstrated how the concept of civilization was deeply informed by changing views on madness (e.g., with the birth of the psychiatric clinic and carceral institutions), Asad examines how the secular is constructed in relation to changing views on religion. As he writes in *Formations of the Secular* (2003):

> What interests me particularly is the attempt to construct categories of the secular and the religious in terms of which modern living is required to take place, and nonmodern peoples are invited to assess

> their adequacy. For representations of 'the secular' and 'the religious' in modern and modernizing states mediate people's identities, help shape their sensibilities, and guarantee their experiences.
>
> (14)

Asad's work helped to move the conversation from thinking about the secular as a natural-historical development toward a focus on how it operates as a doctrine or an ideology that nation-states make use of to shore up power in the never-ending contest to define national and civilizational identities.

We can see the influence and development of Asad's approach with Janet Jakobsen and Anne Pellegrini's 2008 edited volume *Secularisms*. With essays focusing on uses of the secular toward minorities in the United States, as well as in non-Western countries such as Iran, India, and China, Jakobsen and Pellegrini expand on Asad's method by situating the secular in relation to colonial and post-colonial histories. As they write, "If secularism is constituted in relation to religious formations, then secularism is not the universal discourse emanating from the European Enlightenment, but is in fact multiple, as are religions" (13). In this way, 'formations of the secular' ought to be considered in relation to various 'religious formations' – all of which produce distinct modes of belief, practice, and governance. This approach also builds on the influential work of Charles Taylor in his much-debated *A Secular Age* (2007), which provides a detailed investigation of how modes of 'Christian secularism' have cultivated a type of secular subjectivity and thereby influenced how we relate to religion. Most notable here is what Taylor calls secularity 3, which he describes as "a move from a society where belief in God is unchallenged and indeed, unproblematic, to one in which it is understood to be one option among others, and frequently not the easiest to embrace" (3).[10]

In their edited volume *Secularism and Religion-Making* (2011), Markus Dressler and Arvind Mandair categorize three different strands of scholarship that have sought to problematize the secular, including the "secular liberal" philosophy of thinkers like Charles Taylor; postmodernist critiques coming from Continental philosophers and political theologians looking to re-engage religion as a source of meaning (typically liberal interpretations of Christianity); and those associated with the work of Foucault and Edward Said, who rely on discourse analysis to critique formations of the secular in the tradition of Talal Asad (4). The first two schools of thought tend to hold the view that "there is an essentially historical difference between the West and the non-West," while the latter calls this division into question.

Central to Dressler and Mandair's thesis is the influence of three key figures – Luther, Kant, and Hegel – who deeply influenced Western conceptions of the secular. This includes a turn toward individualism with Luther (e.g., a focus on the relationship between the self and God); the distinction between faith and reason with Kant, where reason preserves faith's integrity by placing it in a separate domain of thought; and the ability of traditions to take a critical view of their own origins and meaning with Hegel (7). As an alternative to these traditions, Dressler and Mandair propose the following:

> What tends to be conveniently omitted (or repressed) in the recounting of Europe's intellectual and cultural history is the memory of imperialism as an event that might have influenced the development of critical thinking and cultural identity of the West (Europe and North America). Our argument is that modern intellectual history, the development of its thought process, is inextricably linked to the history of its encounters with non-Christian cultures, which can by no means be limited to the encounter with Islam and the Crusades.
>
> (8)

For Dressler and Mandair, there is no way to separate Europe's colonial-imperial adventures circa 1492 from the construction of secularism (and thus religion) since they are events that occurred more or less simultaneously. For example, they suggest that Luther's rejection of the Catholic dogma "in loving God one should also love God's creatures" is tied to historical developments that uphold the ideal of an autonomous, reasoning individual as the true path toward salvation. This individualist ethos informed (and was later influenced by) colonial encounters and the many 'civilizing missions' that followed. As they put it, "The contours of the West and the non-West were thus codependent and co-emergent, that is, mutually fleshed out (translated) within this model of self-representation" (10). From this, it follows that the very idea of secularization was and remains caught up in colonial processes that continue to inform our laws, institutional structures, and cultural sensibilities.

Taking these points further, Jonathon Kahn and Vincent Lloyd (2016) note that "secularism as a response to religious strife or, better, as a response to strife attributed to religion has no necessary connection with one place and time." For this reason, they argue that "[t]here is no need to take European intellectual history as paradigmatic." Instead, they urge scholars to address secularism "not just as the management of discourse but also as the management of practices and bodies, not just as an elite exercise or power but also as the management of lives of ordinary people" (6). These points will be taken up in chapter 2 when I discuss the ways in which certain religious symbols, such as the hijab and niqab, are deemed threatening to 'secular values.'

Ultimately, Dressler and Mandair argue that scholars should move beyond Asad, who in their estimation "comes tantalizing[ly] close to acknowledging the nature of contemporary religio-secular as an aporia, an irresolvable contradiction" but does not push any further (18). What, then, does going beyond Asad look like? Here they draw on Ananda Abeysekara's concept of "un-inheriting" the very idea that there is a solution to the religion/secular binary and instead suggest that we live with the contradiction and focus our efforts on theorizing how religion is discursively produced in relation to secularism and vice versa (19). They also suggest distinguishing between three different types of religion-making: *from above*, where religion is used to legitimate certain types of power (e.g., government); *from below*, where subordinate groups draw on common "religionist discourse" to legitimate their identities; and *from (a pretended) outside*, by which they mean uncritical scholarship that mimics the first two categories and thus adds to the perception that they are somehow natural or real (21).

In this book, I will be primarily concerned with exploring the interrelationship between religion- and secular-making from above and below. Following Asad's critique of Habermas (see introduction), I am particularly interested in how religion-making from above rarely engages in anything resembling 'cultural translation,' while religion-making from below tends to privilege those who are able to prove their secular *bona fides* by parroting the language of dominant groups, as when Muslim women living in Western states center the idea of 'choice' when it comes to the wearing veil. In cases such as these, the various cultural, political, and theological reasons for veiling are typically left out of the conversation, thus leaving very little to 'translate' in the first place.

Post-secularism

Precursors to the concept of post-secularism can be found as far back as Andrew Greeley's 1966 essay "After Secularity," which deals with the Catholic Church's post-Vatican II embrace of certain secular principles, such as ecumenicism and evolution. However, it was not until the late 1990s that the term began to take hold, as seen in the work of German sociologist Klaus Eder, who used it to refer to the "resilience of religious beliefs and practices across the world" (Mendieta 2019: 53). Habermas uses the term in his aforementioned 2001 lecture (see introduction) to indicate both a factual recognition that religion is here to stay and a political strategy to get people to think about how we might collectively engage with the apparent rise in religious discourse in the public sphere. A similar sentiment is expressed in Lawrence Sullivan and Hent de Vries's edited volume, *Political Theologies: Public Religions in a Post-Secular World* (2006), which acknowledges their indebtedness to Casanova's *Public Religions in the*

Modern World, and classifies the post-secular as an open terrain of competing ideologies vying for a place in the wake of the post-Soviet and post-9/11 worlds.

One of the best overviews of post-secularism comes from James Beckford's SSSR Presidential Address (2012), which looks at six clusters or common uses of the term within a variety of scholarly fields, including a reaction to the decline in secularization theory; a blurring of lines between public and private, thus calling into question the Protestant-centric separation of these spheres (5); the rise of faith-based organizations in places like Britain; a covert way of bringing "some form of spirituality back into the center of a society's concerns" (11); and more. Beckford's main critique is that the concept of post-secularism "is likely to obfuscate – or divert attention from – questions about the involvement of states in shaping and regulating public responses to religious diversity" (12). As one example of why this concept is misguided, Beckford notes how responses to Muslim immigration in Euro-Western states have led to an increase in securitization and thus heightened the visibility of certain types of religion in the public sphere – a point that I will address in relation to the veil in chapter 2. As another example, Beckford points to the role of neoliberal policies in contributing to the "growing importance" of faith-based organizations as they take the place of social welfare services (15).

Beckford's point here is that the 'post' in post-secular reflects more of a change in public perceptions regarding what *looks* like religion (e.g., the increased presence of turbans and veils) than a useful description of social reality. Indeed, with spikes in immigration coming from the global South, concerns over religious extremism following 9/11, and the decline in social welfare services (and hence a decline in economic security), greater attention has been drawn to how states manage certain types of 'religion' as a perceived threat to national and Western values.

A more recent volume on this topic is Justin Beaumont's *The Routledge Handbook of Postsecularity* (2019), which includes a variety of approaches beyond the usual suspects (i.e., philosophy and theology), including the field of critical political geography. As Beaumont and Klaus Eder (2019) note in their introduction, "Work on postsecularity tends towards a Western- and especially Euro-centrism, and so reaching out to critical scholarship in Russia, India, and Asia on decolonial thought beyond a global development perspective is an important new feature" (8). In this sense of the term, 'post-secularity' reflects a loose and shifting cluster of ideas that attempt to grapple with the blind spots in secularization theory and the crisis in 'secular' liberal multiculturalism. This includes sociological approaches accounting for things like demographic change, theories of political geography that consider how the boundaries between public and private are being redrawn, theological and philosophical approaches toward questions of pluralism and inclusion, and more.

Ultimately, I do not use this term as an analytic concept myself, though I do acknowledge that some attempts to 'own' it can be useful. For example, in his contribution to Beaumont's volume, Øyvind Strømmen (2019) acknowledges that post-secularism "is largely a Eurocentric concept." At the same time, he argues that "it is useful in describing a very tangible change that has taken place within secular European countries in the past few decades, and particularly in the post-9/11 era." For Strømmen, 'post-secular' calls attention to the fact that since 9/11 "we talk more about religion and we speak differently about religion" (396). Pointing out scholarly interests behind this concept does not, of course, undermine certain self-reflexive uses of post-secular, but it does help to historicize the term by focusing on the various political and ideological motivations behind its use.

Realignments

Thus far, I have described some of the main scholarly shifts in thinking about the secular since the 1960s, with particular attention to the post-9/11 period. Chief among these shifts was a rethinking of secularization theory and its loftier predictions about the inevitable decline of religion, as seen with the use of the term 'post-secularism.' If nothing else, this realignment points to a surge of scholarship in response to the missteps of older theories secularization as post-Soviet and post-9/11 political re-formations brought closer attention to these issues, particularly the heightened emphasis on Islam. Indeed, the tendency to reduce the motivations behind the 9/11 attacks to 'Islamic fundamentalism' has contributed to a hyper-focus on religion as a primary explanation for global unrest. Where the secular fits within this matrix is, I would argue, largely dependent on how these terms are redefined in light of world-changing historical events and the corresponding value that nations, organizations, and individuals perceive in embracing, rejecting, or ignoring these labels . . . only to take them up again when the time is ripe. Much the same could be said for terms such as socialism and atheism, the latter of which I will address in chapter 3.

Political secularism and its uses

In her book *Sex and Secularism* (2018), Joan Scott argues that much of the current discourse on secularism can be traced back to certain changes that took place during the Cold War, where the idea of 'religious freedom' functioned as a way to differentiate the capitalist West from the 'godless' Soviet Union. As she writes:

> The relationship of the state to religion was reformulated as the Soviet Union came to represent, not the embodiment of secularism as it had been defined in the nineteenth-century anticlerical campaigns but the home of what was derided as godless atheism. The Christian elements always present in the secularism discourse now came to the fore as the American version of it (state neutrality defined as the protection of religion from state intervention) was increasingly emphasized. In France another notion had long prevailed – the protection of individuals and the state from the claims of religious communities. But even in France at this Cold War moment there was renewed attention to the rights of private religious conscience, something the Soviets were said to deny. (2018: 122)

Here, Scott highlights how 'religious conscience' and 'religious freedom' were used to distinguish competing Cold War ideologies and contributed to the idea that secular liberal democracy was a natural extension of certain Christian ideals. The fact that this also occurred in France – the most 'secular Republican' of nations – underscores the complex political entanglements between secularism, religion, and culture.

In her 2008 book *The Politics of Secularism in International Relations*, Elizabeth Shakman Hurd provides a useful typology for thinking about the political entanglements between religion and the secular with her distinction between laicism and Judeo-Christian secularism. She writes:

> Each of these traditions of secularism is associated with particular sets of practices. Laicism, which comes out of the Enlightenment critique of religion, is associated with attempts to force religion out of politics. The secular spheres are emancipated and expanded "at the expense of a much-diminished and confined religious sphere." Judeo-Christian secularism is associated with attempts to claim and reinforce the 'secular' as a unique Western achievement that both distills and expresses the essence of Euro-American history, civilization, and culture. (22)

While these distinctions could no doubt be further refined, they are nonetheless helpful for thinking about how various Euro-Western states continue to manage or regulate religion in relation to pre-existing political ideologies and cultural practices.

In states like the US, for example, where a Judeo-Christian heritage is often highlighted as part of national or even civilizational identity, secularism tends to be framed in relation to certain values and practices that are deemed an integral part of the social and political fabric. Here we might think of national holidays, the Constitution, or laws on gay marriage and religious freedom (Brown 2019). In states like France and the Canadian province of Québec, secularism takes on a more explicit character as a governing framework to limit the public influence of 'religion,' where an emphasis on laïcité is presented as a unifying ideology *for all* (Scott 2007). In both of these cases, however, the secular functions more as a rhetorical strategy of political power than as a clear set of ideas and principles that can be consistently applied across the board. As John Bowen (2008) puts it in his important study on the politics of the veil in France, "It makes no sense for a social scientist or historian to ask, 'Does this policy reinforce laïcité?' – although it makes great sense for a politician to do so" (2). From this it follows that the political uses of the secular reflect a constellation of shifting variables that are shaped by the interests of political power. For example, Scott (2018) observes how the "substitution of Islam for Soviet communism as a threat to the West at the end of the Cold War" (13) ushered in a different set of variables that became constitutive of the secular, most notably the connection to gender equality. She continues:

> Today, secularism is at the center of arguments about immigrants being advanced by politicians on the right and the left in the countries of Western Europe. In these debates, secularism is identified with Western practices and beliefs that are said to contrast dramatically with Islam; gender equality is offered as one of the defining characteristics of this secularism.
>
> (10)

As will be discussed in chapter 2, the emphasis on gender equality as a central component of secularism is a product of post-Cold War and post-9/11 discourses on Islam and is not a value intrinsic to the secular.[11]

It is also important to note how the use of the secular is expanding among different political groups, including those who have previously ignored or rejected this term when describing their own identity and ideological preferences. As Per-Erik Nillson (2019) observes in his study of the right-wing nationalist group Riposte Laique (Secular Retort) in France, "Secularism is, in this regard, a spectacular category; it becomes a desired object as well as the projection surface for a wide variety of political and social struggles" (17).

For these and other reasons, I follow thinkers such as Bowen, Nillson, and Scott in focusing on the "discursive operations of secularism, its history, and its contemporary political uses" (Scott 2018: 7).

An interlude on the idea of Western civilization

Edward Said's ground-breaking 1978 book *Orientalism* is rare among academic texts not only for remaining relevant forty-plus years after its initial publication but also for challenging reigning orthodoxies in Middle Eastern and Islamic Studies and spurring a variety of related developments, such as the field of post-colonial studies, studies of race and representation, journals such as *Re-Orient*, and the ever-growing number of essays and books dealing with the topic of Islamophobia (Shryock 2010; Beydoun 2018). As Aaron Hughes puts it:

> Said set out to show that the language and categories supplied by *all* nineteenth and early twentieth-century literature, scholarship, and art dealing with the Orient was an attempt on the part of Europe to articulate and better define itself and its values in the light of this perceived Other.
>
> (2016: 42)

While Said was not the first to make these observations, especially when it comes to the topic of Islam and the West, he did so in a way that was novel, and during a time where the social, political, and scholarly milieu was ripe for such an intervention.[12] As Dietrich Jung observes, Said's book "was the learned polemic of a 'Western scholar with oriental roots,' voiced in the new language of post-structuralist literature and surfing on the waves of Third-Worldism" (2011: 17). While Jung does not elaborate on what he means by "post-structuralist literature," Hughes characterizes this approach as a call for scholars and commentators to be more "self-reflective and self-conscious of the language we use" (2016: 43). More specifically, as Said himself writes, his work attempted to highlight the role of culture in perpetuating popular images and ideas (e.g., in literature and art) that led to a "cultural hegemony" on representations of the so-called Orient (1985: 7). In addition, Daniel Varisco (2017) points out that Said's focus on "the checkered history of European imperialist representation and colonialist penetration into the Near, Middle and far[thest] parts of the East" helped to show how Orientalist representations "played a discursive role in the sins of Western history" (6).

Taken together, these observations highlight how the reception of Said's theory brought attention to the ways in which Euro-Western literature, art, and, to a certain extent, scholarship have constructed and perpetuated a repertoire of stereotypes contributing to the essentialization of differences between the so-called East and West. As Varisco's comments suggest, such images played a significant role in creating conditions that would justify colonial and imperial interventions, as seen with the recurring trope of oppressed women in need of saving from barbarous 'Oriental' men (see chapter 2). To be sure, many critiques of orientalist representations in art, literature, film, and TV that were inspired by Said are still relevant today (Shaheen 2014); however much scholars have nuanced and modified his particular conclusions (Varisco 2017). And while there is a lot to critique when it comes to Euro-Western scholarship on the 'Orient,' it is useful to pause for a moment and mark a few key distinctions between popular and scholarly representations to clarify my own reasons for engaging with this theory.

In "Orientalism Reconsidered," Said (1985) admits to certain shortcomings in his work, such as a lack of focus on gender and Black/ethnic studies (1985: 91), though he dismisses criticism that he did not deal with German Orientalism as "superficial or trivial" (90). Commenting on Said's dismissal of German scholarship in this area, Hughes writes, "It was the Germans, after all, who were, in the words of Suzanne Marchand, the pacesetters 'in virtually every field of oriental studies between about 1830 and 1930'" (2016: 43). Hughes's concern here is that many have taken Said's critique of popular art and literature, along with certain strains of scholarship (e.g., the work of Ernest Renan) as indicative of *all* scholarship on the Orient coming out of the Euro-West. While it is certainly true that there is no lack of Orientalist scholarly work for us to consider,[13] the tendency to overemphasize *all* scholarship on this topic as hopelessly retrograde is problematic. For one thing, as Varisco argues, not all scholarship on the Orient can be rolled up into this framework of naked racism and imperialism. As he writes:

> Edward Lane's discussion of Egyptians was no longer modern by the time Edward Said read it. Although the book is acknowledged by modern literary critics as one of those "great Orientalist works of genuine scholarship," Said nonetheless trashes it as coming out of the "same impulse" as racist tracts and pornographic novels. The problem is that Said reads Lane contemptuously rather than carefully, failing to appreciate the critical assessment Lane made in the 1830s of earlier stereotypical accounts of life in Egypt. I find it hard to fault Lane's lengthy description of Islam, which is notably devoid of sarcasm or Christian bigotry.
>
> (2017: 34)

So, what might we take from Varisco's analysis of Said's inability to properly contextualize a thinker like Lane and his role in the production of Orientalism? For one thing, I would argue that this example highlights the tendency of polemical tracts like Said's to overstate the case, which, ironically, parallels a lot of what one finds in much of popular culture and popular media. Tim Murphy states the problem thusly:

> Because it takes as its basis, as its guiding principle, the dictates of practical reason, the temporal horizons of the public sphere are much narrower than are those of the sciences. . . . Practical questions demand practical answers, answers which may form the basis for concrete plans which can be realized within a foreseeable time frame. The public sphere is necessarily constituted by these demands, and cannot have the patience to "wait and see," a gesture of deferral which is essential to science.
>
> (2000: 188)

I want to second Murphy's distinction between scientific work, in the best sense of careful investigation and constant revision, and public debate, which is more constrained by such variables as time, space, incentive structures, and institutional biases. By contrast, good science is open to revision and is willing to "wait and see." Indeed, as Varisco further observes about Lane, he "revised his second edition after receiving criticism from others and finding materials he had forgotten at first writing" (35). This is not to suggest that Lane did not contribute to the perpetuation of certain stereotypes, but rather that Said's (important and necessary) polemic often tips the scales in favor of conflict instead of looking for instances of incremental improvement.

Said also fails to deal with what some have called "affirmative Orientalism" (Clarke 1997), which attempted to mount an East/West synthesis, as in the work of Goethe and Louis Massignon. Moreover, Said downplays how the process of scholarly investigation (e.g., through translation, interviews, and textual analysis) is a messy business of discovery through trial and error. To be sure, scholarship is often tied to racial, gendered, colonial, and imperial domination. At its best, however, it contributes to the production of novel ideas that attempt to describe and explain *difference* within human societies. Teasing out these tensions is thus important, especially in our digital media age, where brevity, outrage, and abundance are the norm.

Zachary Lockman offers one example of how we might rethink the politics of Orientalism in his book *Contending Visions of the Middle East* (2004), which begins by deconstructing the popular notion that Europe and the West have an origin in ancient Greece and Rome, and argues that the very idea of 'Western civilization' was a modern invention that only became popular in the nineteenth century. Contrary to claims of Western ownership of this heritage, Lockman looks at how the ancient Greeks and Romans saw themselves, including how they were influenced by and borrowed from various cultures, such as Egypt and Persia. As he writes:

> [T]hough many European scholars would later depict Greek culture in the "classical" period of antiquity as wholly new and unique . . . we know that in fact the Greeks were very much influenced by, and borrowed from, the cultures of their older, richer and more powerful neighbors to the south and east. These included mighty Egypt, the various empires which arose in the fertile and densely populated lands between the Tigris and the Euphrates rivers . . . and the Phonenicians.
>
> (10)

Ultimately, Lockman's study demonstrates how the politics of Western civilizational rhetoric has functioned as a way to demarcate the West from the East, legitimize claims to certain imagined lineages, and justify colonial and imperial wars, along with the inclusion and exclusion of various groups who can be marked on one or the other side of this ledger.

Historical studies like Lockman's underscore how claims to a coherent lineage of Western civilization fall apart upon closer investigation, as Anne Norton (2013) also demonstrates in her analysis of medieval Muslim scholars and their role in the construction of Western philosophy. Studies like these lay bare the impossibility of asserting any clear or coherent notion of Western culture as a trans-historical phenomenon, despite modern attempts to do so. In this sense, the idea of competing or clashing 'civilizations' ought to be viewed as political device whose primary function is to reduce complex and evolving traditions to one-dimensional caricatures and thereby maintain a well-worn wedge in the culture wars.

It's culture wars all the way down

The popular website Wikipedia – often searched though rarely cited in scholarship – attributes the origins of the phrase 'culture war' to the German term *Kulturkampf*, in reference to an 1871–1878 dispute between Otto von Bismark, the first chancellor of Germany, and the Roman Catholic Church. Although this dispute was covered in American newspapers in 1874, it wasn't until over 100 years later, with the publication of James Davison Hunter's *Culture Wars: The Struggle to Define America* (1991) that the phrase gained a foothold in everyday speech. For Hunter, culture wars include disputes over abortion, gay rights, and prayer in public schools being waged between competing groups – one holding progressive and the other holding more orthodox values.

Stephen Prothero picks up this framing in his own, not-so-subtly-titled book *Why Liberals Win the Culture Wars (Even When They Lose Elections)* (2016), which he wrote in response to a controversy surrounding the proposed construction of the 'Ground-Zero Mosque' in Manhattan beginning in 2010. In his wide-ranging analysis,[14] Prothero argues that in most cases, and contrary to popular opinion, it is conservatives who start culture wars because they are "anxious about the loss of old orders and the emergence of new ones" (13). What is more, he claims that "When liberals win – when anti-Mormon violence becomes a scandal or when a gin and tonic ceases to be one – both sides come to accept the new normal and conservatives move on to the next fight" (4).

While Prothero does not name it here, his statement points to another popular term, 'the Overton window,' which was coined by Joseph P. Overton to indicate the current range of acceptable political ideas (spanning from the unthinkable to public policy) in any given society (Mackinac Center 2021). In recent years, this term has been used to describe shifts in public sentiment, where formerly forbidden ideas have become acceptable (e.g., the Overton window has shifted on gay marriage). I will return to this concept in due course, as it offers a useful heuristic for challenging Prothero's conclusions. For the moment, I want to both affirm and contest Prothero's framing of the culture wars and connect it to larger issues surrounding the secular in contemporary Anglo-American culture.

To put the problem plainly: while it may be accurate to suggest that certain controversial issues become more acceptable over time, as seen with views on alcohol, Mormonism, or gay marriage, other issues will often ebb and flow in public opinion and government policy, as seen with laws surrounding abortion (especially in the United States), or even the scapegoating of certain groups of people, such as Muslims. One thing that is missing in Prothero's thesis is a post-structuralist conception of discourse that accounts for the ways that people strategically use language and symbols for different and often contradictory ends. This can be seen, for example, with the tendency to claim that Islam is either a religion of violence or a religion of peace. In the absence of the 9/11 attacks and the enduring 'war on terror,' it is hard to imagine that contemporary classifications of Islam would have nearly as much social currency as they continue to have today. And while it may be probable that certain identities, such as Mormonism in the United States, no longer represent the perceived threat that they posed in the nineteenth century (e.g., with concerns over polygamy), there is nothing to guarantee that Mormon or Catholic identities won't become attached to other cultural and political controversies that could re-signify them as dangers to *some* once again.

Tara Burton (2020) offers a useful supplement to Prothero's thesis on the matter of how we conceptualize culture and identity formation in the age of social media. Turning her attention to the "religious Nones,"[15] Burton argues that they embody "the idea that our lives can and should be customized to our personal interests and wants and needs" (24). These newish constellations are part of what Burton calls "Remixed" culture. As she puts it:

> [T]oday's mix-and-match culture means that the Remixed can get their sense of community from one place (an intense fandom, say) and their sense of meaning from another (social justice activism, or techno-utopianism). They can practice the rituals associated with wellness culture while seeing their purpose as primarily political.
>
> (32)

Burton's point is that the acceleration of these "customized" identities points to a growing gap between the communities that people identify with and the values or principles that they claim to hold. As choice expands exponentially in the virtual realm, so too do the possible combinations of personal identification, while the basis for social solidarity (i.e., a grounding in certain principles connected to powerful institutions, such as churches or trade unions) is arguably less secure than at any time in recent history. Whereas self-described secularist members of American Atheists would have had fewer platforms in which to cultivate their identities in, say, 1995, younger people flirting with nonreligious identities today often do so in relation to a wide variety of online communities, many of which (through algorithmic suggestions on platforms like YouTube) may not even engage with atheist philosophical ideas at all. In this sense, online identity formation is arguably less moored to conventional issues, dogmas, talking points, and principles than ever before.

Burton's conception of Remixed culture and customized online identities complicates Prothero's notion that certain political issues are eventually 'won' through integration and somehow moved beyond. If identity formation is as fluid as Burton suggests, where identification with group X does not necessarily correspond to the adoption of certain values or principles, such as multiculturalism, then the case could be made that the so-called liberal victories in the culture wars are not once and for all events. Perhaps a better way to frame these developments is to characterize them as temporary shifts in the Overton window, where what was once rejected by certain groups (such as gay marriage) is now more acceptable, while other issues (such as gender non-conformity) have gained greater attention, generating newer controversies that continue to unfold in unpredictable ways.

Counterculture and the 1960s

In her book *Kill All Normies* (2017), Angela Nagle makes the case that to understand today's culture wars, including the rise of Donald Trump and the role of online communities in shifting the Overton window on what is considered acceptable public discourse, a more useful metric is needed than traditional left/right distinctions. Instead, she points to the emphasis on *transgression* and *nonconformity* in 1960s countercultures as a through-line linking left-leaning movements *then* with a more right-leaning ethos *today*.

> [F]or the 60s anti-repression cultural politics most closely associated with R.D. Laing, insanity was considered a creative source, a rejection of mainstream norms and a political act of rebellion. The surreal became a pre-rational creative expression. The throwing off of the id that characterized this transgressive countercultural traditional also characterized sites like 4chan, and its culture of trolling and taboo-breaking anti-moral humor, which is often described as insane or unhinged to baffled outsiders.
>
> (31)

Nagle's framing of 1960s counterculture in terms of "anti-repression counter politics" is by no means a comprehensive account of the many currents that circulated during this time in the Anglo-American world. My interest here is not to affirm or deny Nagle's claims but simply to point to some of the more common historical-cultural touch points that still hold currency when we talk about the culture wars *today*.

The 1960s was widely considered an era of experimentation and transgression in much of the Euro-Western world (and beyond), where older, more conservative notions of national, cultural, and religious identity were destabilized and newer modes of expression began to take hold. In this sense, the 1960s continues to animate and frame certain cultural debates such as the emergence of multiculturalism and the fragility of 'Western values.' While it may be true, as Mark Oppenheimer (2003) points out, that "the sixties" is "not a very coherent concept" (3) given the Bohemian countercultures that came before it and the various shifts that occurred in its wake, it is also true that something did happen – "with etiquette, clothes, language, music, and sexual mores" (4) – especially during the period between "the summer of love" in 1967 and Woodstock in 1969. As Oppenheimer further notes, this period also marked a decline for liberal Protestantism in the United States

(9) and a corresponding rise of what is commonly referred to as the 'religious Right.' Much the same can be said in Canada, though in the province of Québec a different story emerges, as we'll see in chapter 2.

Looking back on this time period with the benefit of hindsight, Christopher Douglas (2016) argues that the 1960s can be read through emerging literary figures,[16] whose novels were a reaction against "the vaguely religious liberal consensus on civil rights" (25) that was embodied in Robert Bellah's concept of American 'civil religion.'[17] Douglas suggests that by looking at influential literary figures of this period, one can see that the so-called liberal consensus at the time did not really take hold. What emerged in its aftermath were cultures that had been submerged through colonial and assimilationist paradigms (recalling Dressler and Mandair's arguments) that "asserted equality of race, but not equality of culture." By re-engaging their "pagan" histories, "minority communities could return [to their roots] for psychological, social, and, indeed, spiritual nourishment" (33).

Douglas's point here is that theories of secularization during this time did not pay much attention to literature, especially among minority groups who were laying the foundations for a cultural renaissance (e.g., Native Americans, African and Muslim Americans). Douglas also explores the rise of the 'Christian Right' during the 1970s as a different kind of reaction to "the bland, liberal, civil religion, assimilationist consensus," which "would decisively shape the culture wars in the decades to come" (59). In this sense, one could argue that certain literary authors of this time were more prescient of future trends than most sociologists, who were enchanted by the spell of a rigid secularization theory.

It has also been argued that after the fall of the Soviet Union in the early 1990s and the dissolution of leftist internationalism, which had centered labor and trade union movements as the locus of political power and global solidarity, a slow but decisive shift occurred toward a greater emphasis on 'culture' as the main battleground for liberal-left political movements. This was true both of party politics and academic life, where Marxist-inspired ideologies (e.g., the study of class and political economy) waned, while cultural studies of various kinds largely took their place (Reed Jr. 2001). This liberal-left turn toward culture was forcefully confronted by many on the political right (along with many self-described liberals), who viewed these changes as a threat to their conception of Western civilization.

To this day, many on the right side of the political spectrum still harken back to the 1960s as the moment when traditional values were first unsettled, as seen with the Nativist warnings of former presidential contender Pat Buchanan, whose 1992 speech at the Republican National Convention is widely considered a flashpoint in the culture wars. Buchanan later elaborated on his argument in his book *The Death of the West* (2001), which pointed a finger at the influence of the Frankfurt School in America during the 1960s (among other factors such as immigration and homosexuality) as harbingers of moral decay.

The clash of civilizations (?) and the pivotal 1990s

By the early 1990s, the Soviet Union was a thing of the past, the children of 1970s immigrants from non-European nations were making their voices heard, and the state of academic scholarship was pushing the boundaries of the traditional canon with the rise of gender, queer, and ethnic studies. It was also around this time that Kimberlé Crenshaw coined the term 'intersectionality' (in 1989), and Allan Bloom penned his book *The Closing of the American Mind* (1987), which was a reaction to the influence of social movements coming out of the 1960s, as well as theoretical developments such as post-structuralism. In Bloom's view, attempts to deconstruct the canon degraded the "great books" of Western thought and promoted moral and social relativism.

A 2.0 version of this thesis was penned in 2018 with Jonathan Haidt and Greg Lukianoff's *The Coddling of the American Mind*, where they argue that younger generations (especially left-leaning college students) have become hyper-sensitive, due largely to the failures of earlier generations to instill in them the virtues of free speech and open–ended debate. Like Bloom, Haidt and Lukianoff tend to caricature their opponents by presenting the worst excesses of these ideas as the norm, while overlooking the more thoughtful scholarly (and activist) iterations of the very theories that they are critiquing. Ultimately, Haidt and Lukianoff offer little more than a defense of the status quo, while claiming the ground of rational, secular reason.

Beyond the apparent ideological chasm that these disputes reveal, where scholars critical of cultural and epistemological change fail to accurately distill what is at stake in broader social, political, and economic terms (opting instead for a catastrophizing rhetoric of moral relativism run amok), these examples do point to a time of transition. This includes transitions both political (i.e., the temporary triumph of liberal democracy in the 1990s) and cultural, as seen with trends in higher education that have pushed the boundaries of what constitutes 'Western culture.' It was also during this time that attention shifted in the Euro-West from the Soviet threat to the perceived threat of Islam, which was catalyzed during the first Gulf War (1990–1991) with the idea of a 'clash of civilizations.'

Although it was Samuel Huntington who popularized the phrase the 'clash of civilizations' in his best-selling eponymous 1996 book, it was originally coined by Orientalist scholar Bernard Lewis in 1990 in an essay titled "The Roots of Muslim Rage." Here Lewis draws on elements of secularization theory, such as the idea that the separation of Church and State is the benchmark for civilized societies and is one that the 'Muslim world' has failed to achieve. As the title of his essay indicates, Lewis's main concern is with the supposed rise in hatred toward the West, as when he writes:

> At times this hatred goes beyond hostility to specific interests or actions or policies or even countries and becomes a rejection of Western civilization as such, not only what it does but what it is, and the principles and values that it practices and professes.
>
> (48)

Lewis goes on to reproduce a number of anti-Muslim tropes, such as the idea that Muhammad's military involvement reflects the inherent violence of the 'Muslim mind' (49). He also wonders why anger toward the West continues to persist since its legacy of colonialism has mostly been "abandoned and resolved" (52) and notes that while "sexism, racism, and imperialism" still exist in the West, these are universal human problems that the West has done more than any other "civilization" to have "recognized, named, and tried, not entirely without success, to remedy" (53). Ultimately, Lewis's argument is an apologia for Western colonialism and imperialism. By framing grievances stemming from ongoing political conflicts as remnants of the past, Lewis implies that ressentiment over material relations (including foreign control over resources, elections, and wars of aggression) is little more than a fiction of the 'Muslim mind,' which is bent on revenge and domination in the name of Islam. Put differently, Lewis portrays the 'Muslim world' as lagging precisely because it has not embraced secular, liberal, capitalist reason.

For Huntington (1993), the clash of civilizations is understood as a clash of cultures that have come to replace the Cold War ideology of capitalism versus communism. For him, future conflicts will take place "between nations and groups of different civilizations" (22), which he classifies as "Western, Confucian, Japanese, Islamic, Hindu, Slavic-Orthodox, Latin American, and possibly African" (25). What is of particular concern for Huntington is that these new identity formations – described as cultures and civilizations – are more central to people's core identities than Cold War ideologies ever were and are thus harder to challenge:

> The people of different civilizations have different views on the relations between God and man, the individual and the group, the citizen and the state, parents and children, husband and wife, as well as differing views of the relative importance of rights and responsibilities, liberty, authority, equality, and hierarchy.
>
> (25)

Like Lewis, Huntington follows a standard model of secularization theory where the West rests unequivocally at the apex of civilization. Such views not only relieve purveyors of a narrow Western-centrism of questioning their own ideological biases (and fragilities) but also function to legitimate normative values, laws, and institutions without having to confront the challenges of cultural difference in a serious way. Like Bloom, Haidt, and Lukianoff, this approach is reactionary and assimilationist, where 'good' and 'bad' Others are measured by how well they have incorporated normative views of Western secular reason.

In a response to Lewis and Huntington, Tariq Ali (2003) reframes conflicts in the post-9/11 period as a 'clash of fundamentalisms,' referring to the Manichean ideologies of both bin Laden and the Western alliance represented by George W. Bush. Ali highlights the West's support of various Islamist groups throughout the Cold War in the fight against communism, and thereby locates current conflicts as a product of historical-political choices (e.g., empowering groups like the Taliban for short-term gain) and not the result of some putative 'Muslim mind.' Whatever else we might make of Ali's arguments, his focus on the ways in which history and material conditions shape ideology provides a more analytically stable basis for understanding the production and influence of various political theologies coming out of the so-called Muslim world.

While there is not enough space to dig deeper into the connections between secularization, civilizational rhetoric, and the current culture wars, the influence of Lewis and Huntington in shaping how ongoing conflicts are framed (e.g., as a struggle between *more* and *less* civilized cultures or civilizations) has arguably come to be the dominant lens through which secular ideologies continue to interpret and manage difference. Mahmood Mamdani (2004) refers to this shift as the triumph of "culture talk," where conflicts that had previously been framed in terms of ideology (i.e., capitalism versus communism) and/or race have increasingly stressed civilizational differences as the main cause of global conflict, thereby placing them outside of history. Taking this point further, Rogers Brubaker (2017) characterizes rhetorical shifts in the post-9/11 period as moving from nationalism to what he calls "civilizationalism" in response to the perceived threat of Islam. This focus on Islam, he writes, has "given rise to an identitarian 'Christianism,' a secularist posture . . . and an ostensibly liberal defense of gender equality, gay rights, and freedom of speech," even by parties "often characterized as 'extreme right'" (1193). As previously noted in reference to Nilsson's (2019) work on the French organization Riposte Laique, such political and cultural realignments are increasingly common today, especially in online spaces where variety and tribalism thrive.

The rise of the trolls: online cultures and 'Western civilization' 2.0

The politics of *transgression* that Angela Nagel links to online cultures like 4Chan has, since the election of Donald Trump, largely been associated with the cultural right, which includes a broad spectrum of extremist ideologies, such as ethno-nationalism and the 'alt-right' (Hawley 2019). This also includes more mainstream categories such as the 'alt-lite,' which distinguishes itself from the alt-right by embracing basic liberal rights under the banner of an unapologetic 'Western chauvinism,' while also railing against Islam and the scourge of political correctness and the so-called cancel culture stifling free speech (Stern 2019). On the left side of the cultural spectrum, Nagel argues that dominant trends have tended to favor a virtue-signaling moralism, as seen on websites like Tumblr and embodied in the term 'social justice warrior.' While I will argue that both of these characterizations are overdetermined, Donovan Schaefer (2019) offers a useful insight for thinking about common forms of identity politics on the left side of this spectrum when he writes:

> Progressive politics, in particular – the politics of antiracism, gender emancipation, queer emancipation, and of new horizons of political enfranchisement – is organized around a retaining and a retrenching of bodies. Therefore, progressive politics is a project intimately associated with shame.
>
> (6)

In other words, this type of left-leaning cultural politics tends to be framed around provoking emotions such as shame and guilt since it relies on a recognition of the culpability that Euro-Western culture (especially white and Christian) have played in the perpetuation of social and structural inequalities. Similarly, Mark Fisher (2013) argues that whereas "class has disappeared" from left-leaning politics, "moralism is everywhere, where solidarity is impossible, but guilt and fear are omnipresent." While this type of moralizing politics is clearly persuasive for some, it can also have the effect of provoking reactionary responses, thereby further entrenching already existing tribalisms.

While I find these left/right categories to be overdetermined as they are typically used to define a far-too-broad array of ideas and ideologies, these distinctions do reflect a common mainstream interpretation of intra-cultural conflicts that are usually framed along these axes. One thing that many agree upon is that the election of Donald Trump was a tipping point, where previously marginal political positions on the cultural right have gained greater support, as seen with the rise of QAnon and the outright dismissal of the results of the 2020 US presidential election by millions of Americans.

Growing distrust in secular liberal multicultural democracy (Brubaker 2017) can be usefully thought about in relation to the confluence of two key variables – neoliberalism and social media. Since the 9/11-attacks there has been an increased sense that liberal democracy is in a state of crisis. Contrary to the optimism of the immediate post-Cold War period, where thinkers such as Francis Fukuyama and Thomas Friedman proudly declared that we had reached the 'end of history,' and that 'the world is flat,' signaling the triumph of neoliberal capitalist democracy and free market globalization, events such as the protracted 'war on terror' (2001–) and the economic crisis of 2008 have significantly undermined such predictions, to say nothing of the Covid-19 pandemic and its ongoing impacts. These structural changes and crises have weakened the legitimacy of secular liberal orders more than at any time since the early 1990s, when it seemed to many that these modes of economic and political governance had triumphed.

For Wendy Brown (2019), the effects of neoliberalism, which she describes as "a bundle of policies privatizing public ownership and services, radically reducing the social state, leashing labor, deregulating capital, and producing a tax-and-tariff-friendly climate to direct foreign investors" (17), are about more than changes in economic policy. Neoliberalism, she writes, is also "a moral-political project that aims to protect traditional hierarchies by negating the very idea of the social and radically restricting the reach of democratic political power in nation-states" (12). In other words, this model of governance that has dominated the globe over the last forty-odd years has undermined older political ideas about the commonweal as "market principles become governing principles" (19) and competition reigns supreme. To the extent that Brown's thesis is accurate, it points not only to a loss of faith in the commons as a space for enhancing social democracy but also to a reorientation toward market logics, including precarious, noninstitutional employment (and thus a degeneration of the workplace as a form of community) and high-risk, techno-utopian solutions to problems ranging from climate change to free speech (see Marantz 2019).

Second, the rise of social media and the ability of previously marginalized voices to enter into the fray of public discourse has created what David Taras calls "media shock," referring to "the magnitude and jolt-like force of media change" (2015: 3), which continues to develop in myriad and unpredictable ways. This change or "shock" has been multidirectional and is far beyond the scope of this book to account for. One thing that seems apparent, however, is that the social effects of this new(ish) media landscape have been highly mixed, birthing both "networks of outrage and hope" (Castells 2012) – such as the Arab Spring, the Occupy movement, and Black Lives

Matter – as well as a surge of authoritarianism, ethno-nationalism, and everything in between.

Indeed, the optimism of the early 2010s, where new technologies were said to be "breaking down social barriers" and creating "an ethos of collaboration and transparency" (qtd. in Nagle 2017: 10), quickly saw digital activist movements for government and corporate transparency, such as Anonymous and Wikileaks, fall into dissolution and, in the case of Wikileaks founder Julian Assange, exile and possible extradition to the United States. Much the same can be said for the Arab Spring, which has not blossomed into some Twitter-led democracy as initially hoped for, but has rather given rise to increasing war (e.g., in Syria and Yemen), and decreasing adherence to international law in places such as Saudi Arabia, Israel, and Iran.

I suggest that the confluence of these two major variables – an erosion of trust in neoliberal democracy (without anything substantive to replace it) and the chaotic and contradictory impact of social media – have had the effect, on the one hand, of destabilizing any secure sense of what Western civilization and values look like apart from rhetorical appeals to one's tribalistic preferences, and, on the other hand, of creating more space for experimentation when it comes to questions of individual and group identity. This latter point, as I will address in chapter 3, is far more fluid and ambiguous than is often accounted for. Where the secular factors in when it comes to questions of identity is less obvious than it may appear.

Hate Inc.

In *Hate Inc.* (2019), journalist Matt Taibbi builds on the influential propaganda model of Noam Chomsky and Edward Herman in their 1988 book *Manufacturing Consent*. In laying out the theoretical backbone of his argument, Taibbi notes three "massive revolutions" that have occurred in media since 1988 that changed the way Americans consume and relate to the news. The first revolution was the ascendency of "conservative talk radio and Fox-style news products," which prioritized opinion over objectivity and "presaged an atomization of the news landscape under which each consumer had an outlet somewhere to match his or her political beliefs." The second revolution was the invention of 24-hour cable news stations, which "trained reporters to value breaking news, immediacy, and visual potential over import" and "created in consumers a new kind of anxiety and addictive dependency" to know what's happening at all times. The third and final revolution was the eventual supremacy of the Internet, which, by the turn of the 2010s, saw a massive concentration of digital platforms "accelerating conformity and groupthink in ways that would have been unimaginable in 1988" (14).

In addition, Taibbi argues that media moguls like Rupert Murdoch "smashed" the framework of the monotone, old-school anchorperson by elevating media personalities like Bill O'Reilly, who were "pointed, opinionated, and nasty" (16). This template, according to Taibbi, paved the way for a counterresponse in more liberal media, which led to the organization of "demographic silos" where the media's primary modus operandi became "intramural conflict" between competing political and cultural identities. If this model is in any way accurate when it comes to mainstream media, it is even more evident online.

Along with Nagle, scholars such as Witney Phillips (2015) have conducted studies on the rising influence of online trolling cultures, especially those that developed on web forums like 4Chan and Reddit, with the basic premise that the politics of transgression, which is a form of cultural capital on these sites, has migrated into popular culture. Phillips argues that there is a symbiotic relationship between trolls (broadly defined as people who engage in transgressions intended to shock) and mainstream culture. Despite some of the ways that trolling has become mainstream, as witnessed by Donald Trump's use of Twitter (Ott & Dickinson 2019), Phillips argues that it is hard to determine whether "a given act of trolling is inherently political, or even politically motivated" (6). What is important is that "trolls are born and embedded within dominant institutions and tropes," and their behavior is "par for the mainstream discourse" (11). In other words, trolls can be interpreted as trickster figures in that they are able to weaponize weaknesses in mainstream culture, including "biases, hypocrisies, and deep inconsistencies" (135), and by replicating "behaviors and attitudes that in other contexts are celebrated" (168) – from cheerleading wars of aggression to promoting selectively narrow outrage.

In his multi-year investigation of online extremists and techno-utopians, Andrew Marantz (2019) makes the claim that "For a long time – for a period, to be precise, that began in the 1960s and ended abruptly on November 8, 2016 – Washington insiders from both parties tacitly agreed on a set of commonsense assumptions." While some of these older "commonsense assumptions" may be out of vogue for a growing number of people, it is not at all clear what has taken their place. As Marantz observes, for a growing number of political actors, ethics and ideology have little purchase. What is important is the aesthetics or appearance of being nonconformist (e.g., transgressive) – whatever that might mean in a particular cultural and historical moment (24).

Marantz spent several years interviewing and traveling to events featuring self-described alt-right, alt-lite, and related movements and figures (such as Proud Boys founder Gavin McInnis) and found that the only clear commonality among them was support for Donald Trump's willingness to blow up the veneer of 'political correctness.' For this reason, Marantz argues that such figures are perhaps best described as "metamedia insurgents," who "[speak] the language of politics, in part, because politics was the reality show that got the highest ratings" (18). In addition, the techno-utopians of Silicon Valley, who have gained untold power following Mark Zuckerberg's mantra that progress is best served when we 'move fast and break things,' have filled the space once occupied by the public sector with the utopian hope of technological solutions (Zuboff 2019).[18]

Studies such as these are by no means definitive accounts of the various structural changes that have taken place over the last twenty to thirty years. They do, however, point to a variety of uncertainties and instabilities that, when combined with the tendency of social media to accelerate outrage and an abundance of information, make it arguably harder than ever before to diagnose what might constitute shared values, identities, interests, and so forth. How the secular will be re-imagined out of this maelstrom in five, ten, or twenty years down the road is anyone's guess, though paying attention to its dominant currents and undercurrents can at least provide some tools to navigate this uncharted territory.

Notes

1 The Oxford English Dictionary provides a similar definition dating back to the thirteenth century, where "secular priests" are those who have left the cloister to live among laypeople (qtd. in Scott 2018: 11).
2 See chapter 3 of Cavanaugh's *The Myth of Religious Violence* (2009) for a thorough critique of this idea.
3 As Scott (2018) points out, laïcité was first used in France in 1871 during the Third Republic "as a challenge to the cultural authority of organized Christianity and to its ability to influence or rival state power" (2018: 11).
4 See Masuzawa's (2005), and Arnal and McCutcheon (2015), particularly chapters 7 and 8.
5 Similar distinctions between political and worldview secularism can be found in the work of Baker and Smith (2015) and Mahmood (2015).
6 Connolly questions this concept in *Why I'm Not a Secularist* (1999), arguing that secularism's claims to neutrality mask the ways in which forms of Western rationality carry "metaphysical baggage" that foreclose "a public ethos of *engagement* in which a wider variety of perspectives . . . inform and constrain each other" (5).
7 One of the more common indicators that are used in support of secularization theory is the declining power of religious institutions, though as Berger observes these influences can sometimes take "new institutional forms," adapting rather than disappearing altogether.
8 See Martin's 1969 *Religious and the Secular* and Greeley's 1972 *Unsecular Man: The Persistence of Religion.*
9 For a critique of rational choice theory in the study of religion, see Goldstein's *Marx, Critical Theory, and Religion: A Critique of Rational Choice* (2009).

10 The influence of "secularity 3" can be seen with the popular academic website *The Immanent Frame*. Other volumes building on and critiquing Taylor's book have expanded the conversation to fields beyond religious studies and political philosophy, including literary studies and international relations. See Warner, VanAntwerpen, and Calhoun (2010), Calhoun, Juergensmeyer, and VanAntwerpen (2011). For a critique of Taylor's model focusing on questions of race in the US, see Kahn and Lloyd (2016).
11 As Scott elaborates, "I was reviewing the rulings on applications of the law, offered from 1905 to 2005, by the French Conseil d'État (France's highest administrative court, whose task is to deal with the legality of actions taken by public bodies). From 1905 until 1987, the court assumed that the question of religion had little bearing on the "woman question" (2018: 16).
12 For example, Norman Daniel's *Islam and the West: The Making of an Image* was originally published in 1958.
13 See Masuzawa (2005), especially chapter 6.
14 Chapters feature cultural clashes ranging from the eighteenth to twenty-first centuries and include debates over Thomas's Jefferson's theological views, anti-Catholicism, anti-Mormonism, alcohol prohibition, and contemporary issues, with a focus on Islam.
15 For a discussion on the category Nones, see chapter 3.
16 Such figures include Toni Morrison, Alice Walker, Ishmael Reed, N. Scott Momaday, Frank Chin, and Oscar Zeta Acosta.
17 According to Bellah, this idea included a general public ideal of adherence to "the existence of God, the life to come, the reward of virtue and the punishment of vice, and the exclusion of religious intolerance" (2006a: 230).
18 For a critique of these trends, see Shoshana Zuboff's *The Age of Surveillance Capitalism* (2019).

Works cited

Ali, T. 2003. *The Clash of Fundamentalisms: Crusades, Jihads, and Modernity*. London: Verso.

Arnal, W., McCutcheon, R. 2015. *The Sacred Is the Profane: The Political Nature of "Religion"*. New York: Oxford University Press.

Asad, T. 2003. *Formations of the Secular: Christianity, Islam, Modernity*. Stanford: Stanford University Press.

Baker, J., Smith, B. 2015. *American Secularism: Cultural Contours of Nonreligious Belief Systems*. New York: New York University Press.

Beaumont, J., Eder, K. 2019. Concepts, Processes, and Antagonisms of Postsecularity. In: J. Beaumont, ed., *The Routledge Handbook of Postsecularity*. New York: Routledge, pp. 4–25.

Beckford, J. 2012. SSSR Presidential Address Public Religions and the Postsecular: Critical Reflections. *Journal for the Scientific Study of Religion*, 51(1), pp. 1–19.

Bellah, R. 2006a. Civil Religion in America. In: R. Bellah, S. Tipton, eds., *The Robert Bellah Reader*. Durham: Duke University Press, pp. 225–245.

Bellah, R. 2006b. Stories as Arrows: The Religious Responses to Modernity. In: R. Bellah, S. Tipton, eds., *The Robert Bellah Reader*. Durham: Duke University Press, pp. 107–122.

Berger, P. 1996. Secularism in Retreat. *The National Interest*, 46, pp. 3–12.

Beydoun, K. 2018. *American Islamophobia: Understanding the Roots and Rise of Fear*. Oakland: University of California Press.

Blankholm, J. 2020. Remembering Marx's Secularism. *Journal of the American Academy of Religion*, 88(1), March, pp. 35–57.

Bloom, A. 1987. *The Closing of the American Mind*. New York: Simon & Schuster.

Bowen, J. 2008. *Why the French Don't Like Headscarves: Islam, the State, and Public Space*. Princeton, NJ: Princeton University Press.

Brittain, C. 2018. Racketeering in Religion: Adorno and Evangelical Support of Donald Trump. *Critical Research on Religion Journal*, 6(3), pp. 269–288.

Brown, W. 2019. *In the Ruins of Neoliberalism: The Rise of Antidemocratic Politics in the West*. New York: Columbia University Press.

Brubaker, R. 2017. Between Nationalism and Civilizationalism: The European Populist Moment in Comparative Perspective. *Ethnic and Racial Studies*, 40(8), pp. 1191–1226.

Buchanan, P. 1992. *The Death of the West: How Dying Populations and Immigrant Invasions Imperil Our Country and Civilization.* New York: Thomas Dunne Books.

Burton, T. 2020. *Strange Rites: New Religions for a Godless World.* New York: Hachette Book Group.

Calhoun, C., Juergensmeyer, M., VanAntwerpen, J. 2011. *Rethinking Secularism*. New York: Oxford University Press.

Casanova, J. 1994. *Public Religions in the Modern World.* Chicago: University of Chicago Press.

Castells, M. 2012. *Networks of Outrage and Hope: Social Movements in the Internet Age*. Cambridge: Polity Press.

Cavanaugh, W. 2009. *The Myth of Religious Violence: Secular Ideology and the Roots of Modern Conflict.* New York: Oxford University Press.

Clarke, J. 1997. *Oriental Enlightenment: The Encounter between Asian and Western Thought*. New York: Routledge.

Connolly, W. 1999. *Why I Am Not a Secularist.* Minneapolis: University of Minnesota Press.

Copson, A. 2019. *Secularism: A Very Short Introduction*. Oxford: Oxford University Press.

Douglas, C. 2016. *If God Meant to Interfere: American Literature and the Rise of the Christian Right*. Ithaca, NY: Cornell University Press.

Dressler, M., Mandair, A., eds. 2011. *Secularism and Religion-Making.* New York: Oxford University Press.

Fisher, M. 2013. Exiting the Vampire Castle. *Open Democracy*, November 24. Available at: www.opendemocracy.net/en/opendemocracyuk/exiting-vampire-castle/ [Accessed 20 January 2021].

Gorski, P., Altinordu, A. 2008. After Secularization? *Annual Review of Sociology*, 34, pp. 55–85.

Hawley, G. 2019. *The Alt-Right: What Everyone Needs to Know*. New York: Oxford University Press.

Hughes, A. 2016. *Islam and the Tyranny of Authenticity: An Inquiry into Disciplinary Apologetics*. Sheffield: Equinox Press.

Hunter, J.D. 1991. *Culture Wars: The Struggle to Define America.* New York: Basic Books.

Huntington, S. 1993. The Clash of Civilizations? *Foreign Affairs*, 72(3), pp. 22–49.

Iannaccone, L. 2010. Economics of Religion. In: J. Hinnells ed., *The Routledge Companion to the Study of Religion*, Second Edition, pp. 461–475.

Jakobsen, J., Pellegrini, A. 2008. *Secularisms*. Durham: Duke University Press.

Jung, D. 2011. *Orientalists, Islamists and the Global Public Sphere: A Genealogy of the Essentialist Image of Islam*. Sheffield: Equinox Press.

Kahn, J., Lloyd, V. 2016. *Race and Secularism in America.* New York: Columbia University Press.

Lewis, B. 1990. The Roots of Muslim Rage. *The Atlantic*, 266(3), September, pp. 47–60.

Lockman, Z. 2004. *Contending Visions of the Middle East: The History and Politics of Orientalism*. Cambridge: Cambridge University Press.

Mackinac Center. 2021. "A Brief Explanation of the Overton Window." *The Mackinac Center for Public Policy*. Available at: www.mackinac.org/OvertonWindow [Accessed 20 January 2021].

Mahmood, S. 2015. *Religious Difference in a Secular Age: A Minority Report*. Princeton, NJ: Princeton University Press.

Mamdani, M. 2004. *Good Muslim, Bad Muslim: America, the Cold War, and the Roots of Terror*. New York: Pantheon Books.

Marantz, A. 2019. *Antisocial: Online Extremists, Techno-Utopians, and the Hijacking of the American Conversation*. New York: Viking Press.

Masuzawa, T. 2005. *The Invention of World Religions: Or, How European Universalism Was Preserved in the Language of Pluralism*. Chicago: University of Chicago Press.

McAlister, M. 2018. *The Kingdom of God Has No Borders: A Global History of American Evangelicals*. New York: Oxford University Press.

Mendieta, E. 2019. The Postsecular Condition and the Genealogy of Postmetaphysical Thinking. In: J. Beaumont, ed., *The Routledge Handbook of Postsecularity*. New York: Routledge, pp. 51–59.

Murphy, T. 2000. Speaking Different Languages: Religion and the Study of Religion. In: T. Jensen, ed., *Secular Theories on Religion: Current Perspectives*. Copenhagen: Museum Tusculanum Press, pp. 180–188.

Nagle, A. 2017. *Kill All Normies: Online Culture Wars from Tumblr and 4Chan to the Alt-Right and Trump*. Washington: Zero Books.

Nillson, P. 2019. *French Populism and Discourses on Secularism*. London: Bloomsbury Academic.

Nongbri, B. 2013. *Before Religion: A History of a Modern Concept*. New Haven, CT: Yale University Press.

Norris, P., Inglehart, R. 2004. *Sacred and Secular: Religion and Politics Worldwide*. Cambridge, UK: Cambridge University Press.

Norton, A. 2013. *On the Muslim Question*. Princeton, NJ: Princeton University Press.

Oppenheimer, M. 2003. *Knocking on Heaven's Door: American Religion in the Age of Counterculture*. New Haven, CT: Yale University Press.

Ott, M., Dickinson, G. 2019. *The Twitter Presidency: Donald J. Trump and the Politics of White Rage*. New York: Routledge.

Phillips, W. 2015. *This Is Why We Can't Have Nice Things: Mapping the Relationship between Online Trolling and Mainstream Culture*. Cambridge: MIT Press.

Prothero, S. 2016. *Why Liberals Win the Culture Wars (Even When They Lose Elections)*. New York: Harper Collins.

Reed Jr., A. 2001. *Class Notes: Posing as Politics and Other Thoughts on the American Scene*. New York: New Press.

Said, E. 1985. Orientalism Reconsidered. *Cultural Critique*, 1(Autumn), pp. 89–107.

Schaefer, D. 2019. Whiteness and Civilization: Shame, Race, and the Rhetoric of Donald Trump. *Communication and Critical/Cultural Studies*, 17(1), pp. 1–18.

Scott, W. J. 2007. *The Politics of the Veil*. Princeton, NJ: Princeton University Press.

Scott, W. J. 2018. *Sex and Secularism*. Princeton, NJ: Princeton University Press.

Shaheen, J. 2014. *Reel Bad Arabs: How Hollywood Vilifies a People*. Northampton, MA: Olive Branch Press.

Shakman Hurd, E. 2008. *The Politics of Secularism in International Relations*. Princeton, NJ: Princeton University Press.

Shakman Hurd, E. 2015. *Beyond Religious Freedom: A New Global Politics of Religion*. Princeton, NJ: Princeton University Press.

Shryock, A., ed. 2010. *Islamophobia/Islamophilia: Beyond the Politics of Enemy and Friend*. Bloomington: Indiana University Press.

Stern, A. 2019. *Proud Boys and the White Ethnostate: How the Alt-Right Is Warping the American Imagination*. Boston, MA: Beacon Press.

Strømmen, O. 2019. The Nordic Far-Right and the Use of Religious Imagery. In: J. Beaumont, ed., *The Routledge Handbook of Postsecularity*. New York: Routledge, pp. 395–409.

Sullivan, L., de Vries, H. 2006. *Political Theologies: Public Religions in a Post-Secular World*. New York: Fordam University Press.

Taibbi, M. 2019. *Hate Inc.: Why Today's Media Makes Us Despise One Another*. New York: OR Books.

Taras, D. 2015. *Digital Mosaic: Media, Power, and Identity in Canada*. Toronto: University of Toronto Press.

Taylor, C. 2007. *A Secular Age*. Cambridge: Harvard Belknap Press.

Varisco, D. 2017. *Reading Orientalism: Said and the Unsaid*. Seattle: The University of Washington Press.

Warner, M., VanAntwerpen, J., Calhoun, C. 2010. *Varieties of Secularism in a Secular Age*. Cambridge: Harvard University Press.

Zuboff, S. 2019. *The Age of Surveillance Capitalism: The Fight for a Human Future at the New Frontier of Power*. London: Profile Books.

2 The secular and the veil

At the start of a heated election campaign back in 2015, which would see then-Canadian Prime Minister Stephen Harper unseated after almost ten years of Conservative Party rule by a young and telegenic Justin Trudeau, Harper spoke in the House of Commons on maintaining his government's ban on the niqab during oath-taking ceremonies for Canadian citizenship:

> We don't allow people to . . . cover their faces during citizenship ceremonies. And why would Canadians, contrary to our own values, embrace a practice at that time that is not transparent, that is not open and, frankly, is rooted in a culture that is anti-women. Mr. Speaker, that is unacceptable to Canadians, unacceptable to Canadian women.
>
> (CBC Radio 2015)

Harper was responding to Zunera Ishaq, a then-permanent resident from Pakistan who had challenged the Conservative government's 2011 niqab ban during citizenship ceremonies. What followed Harper's speech in the House of Commons was the most heavily publicized single-issue controversy in Canadian politics in recent memory as the niqab took center stage throughout the federal election campaign of 2015.

Commenting on Harper's speech, then-leader of the Liberal Party Justin Trudeau spoke in Toronto in response to the proposed niqab ban, stating:

> You can dislike the niqab. You can hold it up it is a symbol of oppression. You can try to convince your fellow citizens that it is a choice they ought not to make. This is a free country. Those are your rights. But those who would use the state's power to restrict women's religious freedom and freedom of expression indulge the very same repressive impulse that they profess to condemn. It is a cruel joke to claim you are liberating people from oppression by dictating in law what they can and cannot wear. But what's even worse than what they're saying is what

DOI: 10.4324/9781003031239-2

> they really mean. We all know what is going on here. It is nothing less than an attempt to play on people's fears and foster prejudice, directly toward the Muslim faith. This is not the spirit of Canadian liberty, my friends.
>
> (Wherry 2015)

As I followed this story in real-time back in 2015, one thing that struck me was how quickly public opinion in Canada seemed to coalesce around opposition to the niqab, despite the novelty of this issue. Little attention was paid to the initial niqab ban from citizenship ceremonies back in 2011, and there had been no significant discussion about it in Canada up until that time. Although the Harper government managed to stoke a culture war around the niqab, Trudeau's strong opposition to the ban did not cost him the election, and the issue all but disappeared from public attention once his party assumed power in October 2015.

While it may seem obvious to some, it is worth stressing that debates over veiling are never just about the veil itself but also about a host of issues that the symbol in question – be it a veil, a turban, or a cross – comes to signify. How these debates are mediated to the general public depends in large part on the ability of political actors to create "affective points of conversion" (to borrow a phrase from Sara Ahmed) between the symbol in question and competing visions of national or civilizational identity (Ahmed 2004). In Canada, this typically ranges from variations of what Shakman Hurd calls 'Judeo-Christian' secularism (albeit with an emphasis on multiculturalism) to more nativist views, including regionalism (esp. in Québec and Alberta), to outright xenophobia and white nationalism (Wherry 2021).

Prior to the niqab affair, a national conversation was sparked across Canada beginning in September 2013 after the government of Québec (led at that time by the Parti Québécois) proposed a Charter of Values (Bill 60), which aimed to prohibit all public sector employees from wearing "conspicuous religious symbols" in the workplace. Although Bill 60 included a variety of different religious symbols, prior controversies in the province focused exclusively on the veil. Indeed, the initial title of the bill – "Charter Affirming the Values of State Secularism and Religious Neutrality and of Equality Between Women and Men, and Providing a Framework for Accommodation Requests" – clearly highlights this dynamic. That the Parti Québécois later dropped this lengthier title from the bill, and along with it the clear allusion to Muslim women with the reference to "equality between women and men," speaks not only to the initial motivations behind Bill 60 but also, crucially, to how the rhetoric of secularism (or laïcité in French) is often drawn upon to mask Western-centric social arrangements through the language of gender equality and state neutrality. As I will discuss in part four of this chapter, the claim by numerous politicians, pundits, and citizens in Québec that crosses displayed on public grounds are 'cultural' and not 'religious' symbols speaks to this broader phenomenon.

Unlike debates over religious symbols in Québec, Stephen Harper did not make any clear reference to secularism or secular values in his appeal to ban the niqab from citizenship ceremonies. Nor did he appeal to multiculturalism, which the Conservative Party of Canada has tended to view with suspicion (Wherry 2021). Instead, Harper drew upon well-worn civilizational rhetoric regarding the limits or boundaries of what constitutes Canadian and, by association, 'Western' identity. In this sense, Harper made use of one version of 'Judeo-Christian' secularism, including an appeal to gender equality, despite his party's questionable record on such issues (Hamandi 2015). Trudeau, for his part, relied on a more liberal and multiculturalist variant of this same idea, where state neutrality is understood as a vehicle to maximize the legal accommodation of minority practices of various kinds. While civilizational rhetoric and appeals to gender equality were also present with Bill 60 in Québec, the province's eventual decision to restrict all religious symbols under Bill 21 in 2019 presents a more complicated picture of the secular and its political uses.

Both of these cases sparked national and international attention as a Western state (Canada) known for its adherence to multiculturalism grappled in public with the 'reasonable limits' of what it was willing to accommodate under law. Before turning to examine these two cases – the niqab affair and the discourse on laïcité in Québec – I discuss some common representations of Muslim women in the Euro-West since the eighteenth century: in popular culture, news media, and via legal rulings in a variety of European states. Historicizing these common representations of Muslim women is important not only for understanding the inheritance of popular conceptions of the veil in our present moment but also for grappling with the recent emphasis on gender equality as an integral part of the secular.

Some preliminary remarks on the veil

Leila Ahmed's *Women and Gender in Islam* (1992) is an oft-cited book that helped to spur interest in how Muslim societies have grappled with questions of gender, from the ancient world to the present, including the veil. For example, Ahmed points out that the veil was not an Islamic invention but was initially a status symbol in places like the ancient Assyrian, Byzantine, and Persian empires. The fact that veils were often worn by well-to-do women in these times and places (e.g., to avoid the gaze of commoners when entering the public square) raises questions about its uses and its meaning, including the role of social class as a significant variable.

Following the publication of Saba Mahmood's, *Politics of Piety* (2005), topics like Islamic feminism, women's agency, and embodiment have been increasingly popular in studies on the veil. Mahmood's focus on the *practice* of veiling (e.g., how it is embodied and negotiated by those who wear it) helped to shift the discussion away from the veil's relationship to scriptural or patriarchal commands toward a more complex analysis of how women justify its meaning and purpose for themselves. In this sense, Mahmood's work also pushed the boundaries on what it means to be a feminist. Similarly, Leila Ahmed's *A Quiet Revolution* (2011) argues that Islamist movements in places like Egypt have even influenced struggles for gender equality in the United States (and elsewhere in the Euro-West), thus complicating stereotypes about the role and influence of women in Muslim-majority countries.

By now there is such a large body of literature on veiling practices (and women in Islam more generally) that one would have difficulty covering all the relevant topics in a large book-length study. My goal in this preamble is not to pretend that I can reasonably cover this terrain but simply to note how research in this area has been trickling out into popular and political culture for at least the last fifteen-odd years. This growing body of scholarship has demonstrated how the veil is a highly contested symbol that often functions as a stand-in for what it means to be Muslim, and, relatedly, what it means to be modern, liberated, and secular. It stands to reason then, that as the discourse on the veil changes, so too does the discourse on the secular.

In what follows, I build on Joan Scott's (2018) observation in *Sex and Secularism* that "attention to secularism has once again entered popular discourse as part of the 'clash of civilizations' rhetoric" (1). As noted in chapter 1, what is unique about this post-Cold War civilizational rhetoric is how it has latched onto gender equality as a key marker dividing the West from Islam. Like Scott, I am interested in how the elevation of gender equality as a universal marker of secularism functions as a political discourse to reinforce the superiority of the West and the inferiority of Islam. Building on this framework, I examine how contemporary veiling discourses reshape the secular in ways that transcend older left/right, religious/secular, cultural and political identities and argue that the primary political function of the veil in the Euro-West is a symbolic one, where it serves as a stand-in for competing visions of national and, by extension, Western identity.

The veil, gender, and orientalism

In her book *Colonial Fantasies: Toward a Feminist Reading of Orientalism,* Meyda Yeğenoğlu (1998) recalls the following experience:

> Whenever I evoked, in various scholarly meetings and conversations in the US, the power of Orientalism to understand the place the veil occupies in such constructions, I have consistently encountered the somewhat suspicious remark as to whether, by locating the question of the veil within the problematic of Orientalism, I am not overlooking the question of Muslim women's oppression at "home" by Islam and indigenous patriarchy.
>
> (121)

As readers may anticipate, Yeğenoğlu rejects the idea that indigenous patriarchy at "home" (e.g., in Turkey, Iran, and Syria) can be separated from what she calls "Orientalist hegemony" (121). This point recalls Dressler and Mandair's insistence from chapter 1 that constructions of religion and the secular need to be considered in relation to the long history of colonial encounters, where European societies and settler nations such as Canada and the United States began to define themselves in relation to the various Indigenous cultures in their midst. While space does not allow for a detailed description of gender and Orientalism, it is important to touch upon some of the more common tropes that emerged from these colonial encounters, which have shaped ideas, ideologies, and policies surrounding the veil to this day, and continue to inform the discourse on Western civilization and 'secular values.'

One of the most detailed treatments of gender and Orientalism comes from Joseph Massad's *Islam in Liberalism* (2015), where he observes that practices such as widow-burning (*sati*) in India, foot-binding in China, along with child marriage and gender segregation in Muslim-majority societies (e.g., the harem), were commonly used to mark differences between the 'East' and the 'West' during the eighteenth and nineteenth centuries (110). In the case of France, Massad points to the work of Montesquieu, especially his *Persian Letters* (written in 1721), as a formative influence on the development of the trope of the enslaved Muslim woman in French literature. In the case of Britain, he notes how Mary Wollstonecraft reproduced this theme in *A Vindication of the Rights of Women* in order to contrast "Eastern despotism" with the ideal of Western englightenment (Massad 2015: 113).

Such depictions of women as passive victims of male dominance were taken up by artists, travel writers, and others, especially images of belly dancers, sex workers, and temptresses of various kinds. Haddad, Smith, and Moore (2006) note similar themes in nineteenth centuries European culture when they write:

> Descriptions of women focused on their alleged promiscuity, devilishness, and voracious sexual appetites and reduced women to objects

> of sexual desire. Writers such as Gustave Flaubert and painters like Eugène Delacroix frequently portrayed Muslim women as naked or scantily clad, lounging in harems guarded by slaves and eunuchs. (25)

These depictions of 'captive beauty,' often tied to the harem, have been theorized by some scholars as nostalgic objects of male sexual fantasies that produce both desire and revulsion in the viewer, especially when it comes to practices like concubinage and polygamy (Zebiri 2010). Similarly, Yvonne Haddad (2007) notes how prior to the eighteenth century "Muslim women often appeared in romances as the personification of desire," while nineteenth-century depictions tended to view such women as "devilish" and perverse, especially in Victorian circles, thus contributing to the idea that they needed to be saved (258–59).

One consistent and underlying theme in these sexualized depictions was the idea that 'Eastern' and Muslim women represent a threat to Western morality – both in terms of their corrupting influence on men and as an example of the excessive nature of Oriental patriarchy. Importantly, these glimpses 'behind the veil' also contributed to the idea that veiling concealed sinister behavior that was carried out in private. As much of the literature on this topic points out, these examples were often drawn upon in Euro-American societies as a way to validate the superiority of Western cultures and to justify colonial missions to 'civilize' indigenous populations.

Colonial and post-colonial encounters with the veil

One popular example of civilizing missions comes from Leila Ahmed's aforementioned book *Women and Gender in Islam*, where she discusses the case of Lord Cromer, a British ruler of occupied Egypt from 1883 to 1907, who championed the unveiling of Egyptian women and extolled the virtues of Christianity and Western civilization. Cromer's unveiling campaign was all the more striking in light of his role as president of the Men's League for Opposing Women's Suffrage in England (153). By drawing on the rhetoric of women's rights abroad while opposing suffrage back home, Cromer has come to embody an early example of how the veil has been used as a marker of pre-modern or 'uncivilized' society.[1] Joan Scott (2007) observes a similar dynamic in colonial Algeria, where the veil was often drawn upon as a metaphor (e.g., through references to "disrobing, unveiling, and penetration") for attempts to civilize (and subjugate) local populations (55). Crucially, these attempts to unveil colonized populations also influenced how un/veiling eventually came to be seen by some Muslims (e.g., as a sign of modernity or as a symbol of resistance to colonial rule).

The forceful imposition of the veil in places like Saudi Arabia and Iran are among the best-known contemporary examples of forced veiling. What is often forgotten in these depictions, however, is the geo-political context that informed such repressive measures. In the case of Iran, for example, the reign of Reza Shah (1925–1941) witnessed the banning of the chador in 1936, and a process of forced unveiling involving soldiers physically removing women's veils, which caused serious friction within Iranian society and contributed to associations between unveiling and Western imperialism. Indeed, anti-veiling campaigns in various nation-states throughout the nineteenth and twentieth centuries highlight the political nature of the veil, and how it has often been used as a wedge issue in Muslim-majority countries between secular elites and those in the lower and middle classes. As Stephanie Cronin (2014) observes, for nationalist elites, who identified with "European mores" in countries such as Turkey, Iran, and Afghanistan during the 1930s, "unveiling became a key signifier of modernity and a central element in an emerging national character." By contrast, their opponents viewed unveiling as "symptomatic of a loss of cultural integrity and a weakening of religious feeling, the last means by which European power might be resisted" (3). While there is much more to this picture, these brief examples should suffice to illustrate how the presence or absence of the veil cannot be reduced to the influence of 'Islam' or particular theologies alone, but must be considered in relation to a host of variables that contribute to the constant (re-)construction of its meaning.

In addition to these nineteenth- and twentieth-century contests over the veil, the post-9/11 period has also seen what is sometimes referred to as a 're-Islamization' in places such as the United States and Canada, where "an increasing number of young adults (daughters of immigrant Muslims) are assuming a public Islamic identity by wearing a hijab" (Haddad 2007: 253). As I will discuss in subsequent sections, the wearing of the veil by many Western Muslims (typically the hijab) has also been framed as a political act in response to anti-Muslim sentiment and an affirmation of identity.

The veil after 9/11

The aftermath of the 9/11 attacks marked a new phase of interest in Muslims/Islam in the Euro-West, though now with a heightened sense of threat that appeared to fulfill Lewis and Huntington's warnings of a 'clash of civilizations,' which the Bush administration drew upon in defense of its so-called war on terror. Here is it important to consider the affective role that 9/11 and its aftermath played in both reinforcing older tropes and creating newer images of Muslims/Islam, especially when it comes to the veil.

In addition to a rise in narratives about political Islam following the Iranian Revolution (1979), Euro-Western audiences were exposed to images of veiled mourning women during the First Palestinian Intifada (1987–1993), the massacre in Srebrenica (1995), and the Bosnian War (1992–1995). In her study of US newspapers during this time period, Ghazi Falah (2005) noticed two common tropes in stories featuring Muslim women: passive victims or active political agents. Whereas newspaper and media images prior to 9/11 mainly featured women as passive victims, thereby eliciting sympathy for the victims and outrage at the perpetrators, more complex dynamics began to emerge during the 'war on terror,' such as stories linking veiled women to suicide bombing.

Newspaper articles, news commentary, and books abound on the plight of women in Afghanistan following the ouster of the Taliban in October 2001, where the burka is featured as a primary image. According to Falah, veiled women in these stories typically appear voiceless, in the background, and "are used almost exclusively to communicate the abnormality of life in Muslim societies marked by violence, religious fanaticism, and political turmoil" (4391). By comparison, Falah notes that unveiled women in Afghanistan were often central in newspaper articles and were drawn upon as a justification for overthrowing the Taliban regime. In one of many examples from her study, Falah observes:

> *The Plain Dealer* (August 20, 2002) used a photograph depicting the joyous celebration of women's new freedoms in Afghanistan. The caption reads: "Uniformed girls marched alongside male classmates as hundreds of spectators – men in turbans and women with their burqas thrown back – cheered them on yesterday."
>
> (4430)

According to Falah, the Afghan conflict significantly contributed to narratives linking the removal of the veil (namely the burka) with positive sentiments such as liberation, freedom, opportunity, and modernity. By contrast, the presence of the veil conjures up images of Islamic fundamentalism and has been linked to fears of 'sharia law' infiltrating Euro-Western societies from within.

In contrast to narratives about Muslim women as passive victims, Fatah also discusses an important and overlooked image that was common in news coverage of the Second Palestinian Intifada: Muslim women as active political agents. While noting that Palestinian women were often portrayed in a sympathetic light (e.g., as victims of violence), Fatah also points to a number of news stories about mothers justifying suicide attacks committed by their sons and even carrying out such acts themselves starting in 2002. These acts, according to Falah, combined with images of veiled women appearing with machine guns during demonstrations against the US and Western coalition, contributed to a pervasive sense of "the incomprehensibility of Muslim societies" (4495).[2] While it is hard to determine the enduring impact of these particular images, especially as they have not been reproduced in recent years, they nonetheless exist in the un/conscious repository of symbols linking veiled women (particularly niqabis) to acts of violence and terrorism.

Following the 9/11 attacks, Selby, Barras, and Beaman (2018) noticed the prevalence of five main tropes about Muslims in Canadian media. These include the Terrorist, the Imperiled Muslim Woman, the Enlightened Muslim Man, the Foreigner, and the Pious Muslim.[3] While these tropes are consistent with the civilizational rhetoric found in other Euro-Western media, including the United States, they also developed in response to local incidents and thus reflect the particularity of national concerns. In this sense, civilizational and nationalist rhetoric work in tandem, where events happening in other Western countries can stand-in as analogous to what's happening 'here' and vice versa (Perry & Scrivens 2019).[4] In one example, the authors date the emergence of the Pious Muslim figure to debates that occurred in Ontario between 2002 and 2006 on the question of whether the province should permit Muslims to conduct faith-based arbitration law, which became known as the 'sharia debate.'[5] During these debates, fears of capital punishment and the stoning of women created affective links between Islam, women, and excessive piety, despite the relatively modest proposals contained in this legislation – namely, faith-based arbitration in marital disputes.[6]

Selby, Barras, and Beaman also note how the figure of the Foreigner or 'new immigrant' has consistently been attached to the niqab, despite it being worn by a significant number of Canadian-born converts to Islam. Emphasis on the foreignness of the niqab also contributed to the idea of "an outsider bringing a culture clash into the body politic" (53). As I will discuss in more detail later, the niqab became entangled in competing visions of 'Judeo-Christian' secularism in Canada, although with a novel twist. Instead of the faceless, voiceless, niqab-wearing woman, Zunera Ishaq appeared consistently in media for the better part of a year and, eventually, won her court case against the Conservative government of Canada under Stephen Harper.

Post-9/11 representations of Islam were not all negative, however, as Evelyn Alsultany demonstrates in her book *Arabs and Muslims in the Media* (2012). Expecting to see an uptick in stereotypical representations of Arabs and Muslims on US television in the wake of 9/11, Alsultany found that a majority of depictions were in fact sympathetic. In TV series such as *24* and *Sleeper Cell*, Alsultany discovered that the most common plotlines featured 'good Muslims,' depicted as patriotic Americans (often working with the Federal Bureau of Investigation [FBI]), who were willing to fight against 'bad Muslims,' commonly linked to terrorism. This tendency to portray a 'good Muslim' whenever a 'bad Muslim' appears is what Alsultany refers to as "simplified complex representations" (14) – 'complex' because they defy one-dimensional stereotypes of the Orientalist variety outlined earlier, and 'simplified' because they adhere to a narrow and acceptable range of behaviors that align with secular norms and don't question US foreign policy.

The ideal of the 'good Muslim' is also reflected in the term 'Islamophilia,' which presents certain types of Muslims – tolerant, pluralistic, peaceful – as exemplars of *real* or *true* Islam and evaluates others on the basis of their ability to live up these norms (Shryock 2010). These "simplified complex representations" thus idealize certain types of Muslim identity, while obscuring the variety of reasons – political, cultural, racial, or generational – for why Muslims may oppose Western policies, at home or abroad. In this sense, the seemingly sympathetic representations that Alsultany discovered on the US TV shows in the wake of the 9/11 attacks do not tend to present the complexity of Muslim cultures (including veiling practices), but instead prefigure good Muslim behavior as that which keeps religious practices to the private realm and performs patriotic devotion to the nation.

Thus far, I have provided a broad and general overview of common images that have consistently been reproduced in Euro-Western culture about Muslims/Islam, and Muslim women in particular. It should be clear at this point that the veil is a complex, multivalent symbol that is often used as a political football in debates over secularism, liberalism, multiculturalism, and modernity. Elizabeth Bucar (2012) captures this dynamic well when she writes, "what the Islamic veil means is not a question that gets worked out in isolation. Rather, Muslim experiences with specific, concrete, and historical events, including non-Muslim critiques of veiling, influenced the contemporary meaning of the veil" (69). To push Bucar's point even further, I would argue that the construction of the veil as 'Islamic' also depends upon specific contexts of interaction since, as we will see, it has also been framed as a cultural, political, and even a secular object, depending on the situation.

Insiders and the veil

Borrowing a term from Saba Mahmood, Mayanthi Fernando (2014) discusses the role of 'native testimonials' in the discourse on Muslim women in France via best-selling autobiographies of figures such as Irshad Manji, Azr Nafisi, and Ayaan Hirsi Ali. Fernando notes how these figures tend to "portray Muslim culture at home and abroad as inherently undemocratic and misogynist." More importantly, Fernando highlights how these narratives have been "cited by politicians and media pundits as indisputable evidence of Europe's Muslim problem, and they have become key to the propagation and legitimation of a sexual 'clash of civilizations'" (193).

Putting aside how individual readers may interpret these narratives, there is a clear market for insiders' critiques of Islam, which is often weaponized in the service of anti-Muslim rhetoric and policies (e.g., Donald Trump's so-called Muslim bans). These types of narratives rely in no small measure on the long history of tropes (as discussed earlier) that have preconditioned audiences to interpret the veil in particular ways. Other best-selling books, like the autobiography of Malala Yousafzai, have also been marketed to depict a more tolerant and peaceful image of Islam, thus reflecting the other side of the good/bad Muslim dynamic.

At the same time, there is a growing market in some spaces for more nuanced discussions of the veil, as seen with the podcast *Polite Conversations* (to be discussed in chapter 3), on Al Jazeera English's program *The Stream* (YouTube 2013), and in the growing study of fashion and the veil.[7] In these forums, Muslim women from a variety of backgrounds are featured discussing questions of veiling that span a wide spectrum of narratives – including experiences of oppression and liberation, traditional and feminist interpretations, opposition, accommodation, and everything in between.

Despite the growth of these more nuanced examples, they tend to take place outside of the mainstream and thus do not reach a broad audience, unlike sensationalistic stories, such as honor killings and 'sharia courts,' that can be weaponized in the cultural wars. When considering these and related cases, Alsultany (2012) offers a useful framework for thinking about the dominant sentiments that post-9/11 representations of Muslim women tend to produce. Despite the shift toward positive images of Muslims in some news and TV shows, she argues that *pity* and *outrage* are the most common emotions that veiling provokes (especially the niqab), while *empathy* – which I define here as identification with others on the basis of shared language, culture, or experience – is in short supply.[8] In this sense, it stands to reason that insiders' criticisms of Islam that play on pity and outrage are more likely to be elevated in the media over those that promote empathy, contributing to a disproportionately negative valence around Muslim women and the veil.

Some recent veiling bans in Europe

In the summer of 2016, photographs emerged of a woman being forced to remove her burkini (a term for modest swimwear worn by some Muslim women) by four armed police officers on a beach in Nice, France. It was reported that the woman was given a ticket that stated that she was not wearing "an outfit respecting good morals and secularism." Following a series of burkini bans in France, the city of Nice ruled in a tribunal that such 'religious clothing' was unacceptable during a time when the country was facing terror attacks and that the burkini was "liable to offend the religious convictions or (religious) non-convictions of other users of the beach" (Quinn 2016). Stating his support for the ban, former socialist prime minister of France Manuel Valls (2014–2016) remarked that the burkini "is the expression of a political project, a counter-society, based notably on the enslavement of women" and is "not compatible with French values" (Kroet 2016). A number of protests also sprung up in front of French embassies in opposition to the ban, including one in London where a group of Muslim and non-Muslim women denounced it as Islamophobic, and held signs with slogans reading "wear what you want." Among those in opposition to the ban was famed author JK Rowling, who weighed in with a widely circulated tweet that stated: "So Sarkozy calls the burkini a 'provocation.' Whether women cover or uncover their bodies, seems we're always, always 'asking for it'" (Mckenzie 2016).

A number of themes appeared throughout this affair that can be found in other controversies involving the veil, including the invocation of secular morality, associations with terrorism and public offense, and a concern with the oppression of women. What marked this incident as different, however, was a strong counter-narrative spurred by the striking image of a women being forced to remove articles of clothing in public by French police. While this example reflects a limit case of how far a Euro-Western state has gone to enforce 'secular' clothing in public, the primary reasoning among those in opposition to the ban followed a familiar rhetorical appeal – namely, promoting women's autonomy and the freedom to choose. Although pointing to Islamophobia as a significant variable, in this case, is no doubt correct, the rhetoric of 'choice' does little to clarify what is at stake in such debates.

As I will demonstrate later, choice rhetoric enables a plausible case to be made both for and against restrictions on veiling, often ignores the cultural and individual motivations behind women's sartorial practices, and obscures how these controversies function as a proxy for disputes over other things. Left out of the picture altogether is how the framing of these symbols as either religious or secular (or cultural) essentializes the meaning of the veil and reinforces the power of the religion/secular binary in the process. Although choice rhetoric continues to dominate this discourse, certain rulings have begun to show cracks in this either/or logic and forced a rethinking of what is and what is not secular.

It is still commonplace to assume that Muslim women who wear the veil are compelled to do so by non-liberal and non-secular cultures from which they must be liberated. This tendency can be seen among certain liberal feminist commentators (Okin 1999), who make a sharp distinction between gender and culture, where culture – that is, certain types of culture – is seen to infringe upon a person's autonomy and choice and, therefore, must be overcome if gender equality is to be achieved. The enduring appeal of this discourse highlights how Euro-Western critiques of the veil are not only limited to right-leaning commentary, but also appeal to certain liberal and left-leaning sensibilities. However, post-colonial feminists have sought to challenge this idea by framing the veil as a positive choice for Muslim women that symbolizes a rejection of colonialism and patriarchy (Abu-Odeh 1991). As Anastasia Vakulenko (2012) puts it, Islamic feminism promotes the idea that "veiling should be seen as symbolic of resistance to patriarchy . . . and hence as a perfectly acceptable, even commendable, choice" (65).

In these examples, choice rhetoric is drawn upon to either affirm or deny the legitimacy of the veil, with gender equality serving as a justification for both sides of the argument. As readers may anticipate, this presents a logical contradiction: if the veil is both liberating and oppressive, chosen and coerced, then claims that it is either one or the other cannot be logically justified. As pundits and politicians butt-up against these contradictions, it is not uncommon to see practical justifications for restricting or banning the veil emerge, such as security concerns, the need to promote face-to-face communication, or the expressed desire to maintain state neutrality, which occasionally leads to broader bans on all face coverings or even all 'religious symbols.'

Reflecting on these tensions, Joan Scott (2007) argues that the discourse on choice reduces the "complex realities" of veiling to a binary opposition between "individual autonomy and cultural compulsion" (127). For Vakulenko (2012), this rhetoric ultimately puts forward "an inadequate account of agency" (73) since it fails to acknowledge that while choice is conditioned by people's circumstances, it is not entirely determined by them. In other words, people can and do 'choose' in ways that might not be recognizable in Western cultures. Moving beyond the rhetoric of choice has proven a tall order in the Euro-West, especially when considering the power of secular liberal ideologies to interpret unfamiliar cultural practices in self-serving ways when they fall outside of accepted norms. At the same time, changing views on the hijab – especially when contrasted with the niqab – reveal a shift in the Overton window in some jurisdictions on how this 'religious symbol' is perceived.

To restrict, to ban, or to hide the ball?

In a research project sponsored by the European Union, Sauer and Rosenberger (2005) classify legal regulations on veiling by three main metrics: 'established restrictive bans'; 'soft, selective regulations'; and 'no restrictive regulations.' Whereas the first category relates to restrictions in public (e.g., on buses and in museums) and places of work, the second category, 'soft, selective regulations,' typically makes a distinction between hijabs and full-face veils, where the latter are deemed to be more extreme and are often prohibited. These distinctions offer a useful metric for categorizing common restrictions and for locating where the most frequent sites of controversy arise.

Bans and selective regulations have occurred most frequently in schools in countries like Germany (2003), the Netherlands (2003), the UK (2005), and Norway (2005). With the exception of the German case of Fereshta Ludin v. Land Baden-Würtemberg (2003), which focused on a teacher's right to wear her hijab in the classroom, all of these cases involved prohibitions on students wearing the niqab to school, thus reflecting a 'soft, selective regulation.' Justifications from court rulings and in the press in the Netherlands and the UK argued that the niqab prohibited communication, while in the German case the Federal Constitutional Court found no legal basis for prohibiting headscarves in the civil service – though it did state that regional judges would be free to rule in favor of a ban in other jurisdictions throughout the country. In the minority ruling, in this case, it was stated that the headscarf represented the oppression of women and political Islam. In Norway, local authorities deliberated for over a year and, despite being reluctant to exclude pupils from municipal schools on this basis, eventually allowed restrictions on the niqab to proceed. No nationwide ban accompanied this ruling. In Belgium, bans on burkas and niqabs started to be implemented in public places in 2003, with a full ban on clothing 'obscuring identity' passing through the Belgian parliament in 2010. Links to religious fundamentalism, terrorism, and foreign culture were routinely cited as justification in the Belgian case. In 2010, France instituted a 'burka ban,' with a €150 fine for concealing one's face in public, and up to a year in prison if it is proven that a male has forced his daughter or partner to wear a niqab or burka.[9]

While it is not surprising that a self-described secular state like France would implement a nationwide ban when compared, say, to the more limited ban in the UK, which has a tradition of multiculturalism, it is noteworthy that gender equality was used to affirm a woman's right to wear a headscarf in Norway, thus highlighting the variability of this principle across different political cultures. This points to a shift in the Overton window in some jurisdictions, as the hijab has become more assimilated under certain 'Judeo-Christian' forms of state secularism, while the niqab remains a contested symbol.

It is also worth mentioning that Germany follows principles of state neutrality and non-discrimination in matters relating to religion, though it does not define itself as secular and views schools as a place where the country's cultural and religious heritage may be transmitted to students. Germany is thus exemplary in that it does not claim to be neutral when it comes to the state's cultural identity, unlike in France and, as we will see, in Québec.[10] Whatever else one might make of German policies on these and related matters, legal rulings like Fereshta Ludin v. Land Baden-Würtemberg don't require politicians to twist themselves into rhetorical pretzels to justify bans or selective restrictions on the veil on the grounds of maintaining secular neutrality.

Increasingly, nation-states have been subject to criticism from minority communities and their allies, especially on social media, prompting legacy media and government officials to address charges of xenophobia toward minorities such as Muslim women. In some cases, governments have changed their justifications for bans or restrictions to not appear discriminatory, revealing both the influence of oppositional voices and the difficulty of relying on the secular as an arbiter of state neutrality.

A case from Spain

In an essay dealing with 'anti-burka' legislation in Spain, Marian Burchardt and Mar Griera (2019) observe how scholarship on veiling bans has tended to frame this issue as a "misrecognition of Muslim women's forms of piety" (187). Although it is certainly important to consider the role of piety as a key factor motivating the habits of Muslim women, Islamic cultures remain largely misunderstood in Euro-Western spaces and tend to be depicted through "simplified complex representations." In this sense, the recognition of piety and related ideas is a long-term, political goal that does little to help us conceptualize the current public discourse on veiling. For this reason, it is more useful to analyze how Euro-Western states construct the meaning of the veil through legal battles and the public debates that surround them since it is this rhetoric that Muslim women are forced to respond to in their defense . . . if they respond at all.

In 2010, the Catalonian city of Lleida passed a by-law banning face-veils in public, which was initially framed as a way to stop "Islamic radicalization" (Burchardt & Griera: 189). This debate sparked initiatives in other Spanish cities, such as Reus, where the conservative *Partido Popular* proposed a statewide (Catalan) ban on face-veils, which was swiftly rejected by a majority. Returning to enact legislation at the local level, centrist and conservative parties in Reus argued in favor of the ban on the basis of "protecting the 'dignity of woman,'" while left-leaning parties who wanted to avoid "stigmatizing the Muslim community" argued for a compromise position by banning all face-coverings in public buildings (190). The following year, the Catalan conservative party CIU won municipal elections in Reus and approved a twenty-page set of by-laws regulating public behavior, including prohibitions against public nudity, public drinking, and all "clothing or accessories that prevent or hinder identification" (190). Of particular note in the Reus case were the justifications given by competing political factions. As Burchardt and Griera write:

> [I]n Reus, those mobilizing against the prohibition mainly described themselves as "secularist" and as distanced from religion. Radical left activists who declared themselves to be "far from religion" vigorously contested the ban and organized the opposition. In this case, Muslim actors were almost invisible in the media debates as the defence of the right to wear the face-veil in public was carried by a small leftist party (CUP) and social activists. Their arguments were not built on concerns over religious freedom but based on notions of cosmopolitanism and the "right to the city."
>
> (195)

What is interesting to note here is how upholding secularism was not at issue for the leftist CUP, despite their self-described secularist identity. For them, the political memory of the Franco dictatorship (1939–1975) made issues such as "control and surveillance of public space" and the specter of authoritarianism central to their opposition to the proposed ban. By contrast, supporters of the face-veil ban were not self-described secularists, but rather conservative Catholics who framed the issue in terms of integration, where the 'burka' (which was conflated with the niqab) was deemed beyond the pale of acceptable citizenship and framed as a 'cultural' rather than a 'religious' practice. Interestingly, these same conservative Catholic supporters of the ban "defend[ed] the headscarf as a respectable practice of piety and denounce[d] the face-veil as an alien practice that contaminates the 'good' reputation of Islam" (196). Burchart and Griera argue that by classifying the full-face veil as cultural rather than religious, conservatives were able to "protect the existing negotiated order of secularism," where the headscarf was deemed to be "compatible with Western modernity" (196).

A few things are worth underlining in this example from Reus, Spain. First, the initial framing of the issue around fears of "Islamic radicalization" drew upon similar justifications that have been used in other Euro-Western states. One effect of this line of reasoning is that it enlarges the scale of the problem from a national to civilizational one, where:

> the face-veil can be considered as an available symbolic resource in the global arena that can be strategically used to play politics in the local

> scene. The hyper-visibility of the face-veil epitomizes fears of Islamization, and its capacity to arouse strong and visceral emotions affords greater public visibility to the prohibition.
>
> (195)

Burchart and Griera's remarks offer a clear example of how the repository of tropes about Muslims and Muslim women are mobilized on the national and local levels. At the same time, pushback in Reus from the leftist CUP forced a compromise deal where the veil was folded into a general ban on all clothing that hinders a person's identification and encouraged a distinction to be made between the hijab (as religious) and the niqab (as cultural). While this may appear as little more than a regular process of political sparring and compromise, it is often through these processes of changing legal justifications that the contours of the secular are re-imagined. In this case, a conservative initiative to stop "Islamic radicalization" had the corollary effect of making the hijab a more acceptable symbol of 'Judeo-Christian' secularism.

Forums of belief and practice

In her analysis of legal discourses on the veil in Europe, Vakulenko (2012) discusses the role of Article 9 in the European Court of Human Rights (ECHR), which makes a distinction between *forum internum*, the right to have an internal belief in a religion, and *forum externum*, the right to manifest one's beliefs (e.g., through one's clothing and rituals). Under this framework, freedom of religion is primarily defined as the right to hold certain beliefs, while expressions of religion are considered manifestations derived from those beliefs. According to the ECHR, Islamic veiling falls under the category of a manifestation of religion, and is thus not a protected belief, making it more vulnerable to bans or restrictions of various kinds.

Borrowing a concept from Mahmood (2006), Vakulenko argues that the ECHR's classification of the veil reflects an example of 'secular hermeneutics,' which constructs religious belief as a relationship between the subject and a religious text. Following this 'secular' (and Protestant) conception of religion, the individual (as opposed to one's culture or tradition) ought to be the arbiter of interpretation. In this sense, secular hermeneutics attempts to remake religious subjectivities, where symbols like the hijab come to be understood as optional (i.e., a choice). This framing helps to explain why many hijab- and niqab-wearing women draw upon choice rhetoric, despite holding other reasons that are largely unintelligible in Euro-Western spaces.

One example that highlights 'secular hermeneutics' in practice comes from Mayanthi Fernando's important study, *The Republic Unsettled: Muslim French and the Contradictions of Secularism* (2014), where she interviews a number of second- and third-generation Muslims in France. Among other things discussed in these interviews is how Muslim French women who wear the hijab justify their 'choice' in a country that is generally hostile to such practices. As Fernando writes:

> For Muslim French, the veil is both a self-directed choice and a religious duty. An external authority cannot impose veiling, which must be undertaken willingly, according to the dictates of individual conscience. Veiling is also necessary for cultivating the kind of pious Muslim self that religious authorities delineate. However, secular law and public discourse consistently compel Muslim French to categorize the veil as either a choice or an obligation.
>
> (167)

What is important to note here is how choice is conceived of by these particular women, reflecting their negotiation between certain modes of Islamic theology that they deem authoritative and the republican values of the French state.

The point that I want to stress in these examples from various European countries is that secular hermeneutics is unable to recognize the complex, context- and tradition-specific reasons that may lie behind a person's motivations for veiling. Crucial among these overlooked reasons is the way in which many Muslim women conceive of 'compulsion' as a process of embodying certain practices (such as veiling) through repetition and theological reflection. The apparent lack of engagement or understanding of how these common forms of piety relate to what it means to be a 'believing' Muslim is often at odds with contemporary forms of secular hermeneutics that construct gender equality as an expression of individual autonomy, somehow free from the compulsion of culture or religion.

Whether one finds themselves in favor or opposed to these restrictions or bans on certain types of veiling, the secular plays a powerful role in shaping the discourse and common understanding of these 'religious symbols.' In some cases, 'owning' the secular may work to a Muslim women's advantage, as when certain forms of veiling fall under the protection of religious freedom. In other cases, Muslim women find themselves in an impossible bind – forced to defend their sartorial practices in the language of choice while denying additional motivations that in many cases would not be recognized as valid or even intelligible. Cases like these can tell us a lot about Western fragility as they highlight contradictions between stated principles and 'secular values,' and will often make use of minority communities as a scapegoat for deeper conflicts within the body politic. The niqab affair during the 2015 federal election campaign in Canada is a case in point.

Case study: Zunera Ishaq v. Canada

Zunera Ishaq immigrated from Pakistan in 2008, settled in Mississauga, Ontario, and applied for Canadian citizenship in December of 2013. Initially, Ishaq looked for a way around the 2011 policy requiring "candidates [for citizenship] who wear full or partial face coverings to remove them during recitation of the oath" (Fisk 2015) by requesting either a private ceremony or one with only women present. When her request was denied, Ishaq challenged the law, which the Conservative government of Stephen Harper promptly ceased upon as a wedge issue in March of 2015, claiming, among other things, that the niqab is "rooted in a culture that is anti-women." On September 15, 2015, the Federal Court ruled in favor of Ishaq, while the Conservatives filed for an appeal. When the Liberal Party led by Justin Trudeau won the federal election on October 19, 2015, Justice Minister Jody Wilson-Raybould formally withdrew the Federal Court challenge as her first act in office and even called Ishaq to tell her the news on the phone (Crawford 2015). At the time of this writing, Muslim women are permitted to wear a niqab during oath-taking ceremonies for Canadian citizenship.

The Ishaq case parallels many of the themes discussed in the previous sections, particularly the use of 'soft selective regulations' that focus attention on niqab-wearing women. Unlike other cases involving the niqab, however, the Harper government was able to elevate this issue during an election year by framing the question as a referendum on whether this 'religious symbol' ought to part of a ceremony conferring Canadian citizenship. One can hardly imagine a more poignant example of a minor policy dispute transformed into a culture war (e.g., over competing conceptions of Islam, veiling, gender equality, and multiculturalism).

Commenting on the niqab affair, Shelina Kassam and Naheed Mustafa (2017) observed a range of perspectives in Canadian media, including:

> [T]he minority position of 'everybody mind their own business', to 'niqab is awful but I support her right to wear it', to the shriller 'we need to help women who are oppressed', to the openly xenophobic 'if she wants to live that way why did she come to Canada?'. Racist online commentary was not only directed at Ishaq but at Muslims in general. Ishaq and her niqab became the symbol for everything that was wrong and dangerous about multiculturalism.
>
> (81)

One prominent example touching on themes of oppression and xenophobia came from an interview on the Canadian Broadcasting Corporation with ex-Muslim author and commentator Ayaan Hirsi Ali, who stated:

> I do know that there's this split loyalty that is being demonstrated by people who are taking the oath of citizenship of the countries that their parents or they have migrated to, but at the same time their heart and loyalty lies with a competing set of ideologies.
>
> (Nasser 2015)

Hirsi Ali's remarks also recall what Selby, Barras, and Beamen (2018) refer to as the Foreigner trope, which, as previously noted, creates a "conversion point" between the niqab and new immigrants by representing the issue as one of "an outsider bringing a culture clash into the body politic" (2018: 53). In addition, by framing the niqab around competing ideologies or values, the debate becomes focused on what this symbol signifies for diverse constituencies, most of whom have been primed by "simplified complex representations" such as the good versus bad Muslim trope, and not by any substantive engagement with the range of meanings that the niqab may hold in different times and places.

Another example that touches on these themes comes from *National Post* columnist Barbara Kay (2015), who concedes that Ishaq wore the niqab by choice, referring to her as a "sophisticated, empowered niqab-wearer" in contrast to the majority of niqabis, who are forced to wear it. Kay dismisses the idea that the niqab falls under the protection of religious freedom (as promoted by Trudeau, Ishaq, and others) on the grounds that "[v]irtually all Islamic scholars have noted that Sharia does not demand face cover, and that it is usually a regional custom or a diktat by a country's rulers." Kay's affirmation of Ishaq's 'choice' to wear the niqab as an exception to the general rule is an interesting take, and one that is likely informed by Ishaq's numerous public statements (discussed later) expressing her agency. Among other things, this response highlights the dissonance in seeing a niqabi speak, as most commentators are forced to rely on prior scripts (e.g., orientalist imagery) to make their case in such instances. What is perhaps even more interesting is that by invoking the authority of Islamic scholars on the question of the niqab, Kay inverts the familiar discourse of secular hermeneutics. Instead of true or proper religion being presented as an individual choice that is not coerced by religious authority, Kay invokes such authorities to justify her own classification of the niqab as a 'cultural' symbol.

This small sample of narratives in opposition to the niqab highlights the enduring appeal of certain tropes, including the foreigner, the pious Muslim, the oppressed Muslim woman, and a general sense of a culture clash or 'clash of civilizations.' As Kassam and Mustafa also point out, such tropes get filtered through a broader debate on "'Canadian identity,' 'security,' and 'our values,'" including "shared values of openness, tolerance, and gender equality" (76–77). For these authors, the debate over the niqab speaks to the "limits of multiculturalism" and ultimately positions Muslim woman as in need of saving (78). At the same time, Kassam and Mustafa observe how perceptions of veiling have shifted between 2004 and 2014, noting that whereas "hijabs were previously hotly debated, they are now viewed as more acceptable and the debate has shifted to the niqab or full face-veils" (76). As previously noted, this shift in the Overton window highlights the partial normalization of some forms of veiling in Euro-Western spaces and helps to account for the more positive representations (which Kassam and Mustafa do not address) in mainstream media.

Despite the reproduction of numerous tropes about veiling and Muslims in general, most of the media in Canada were sympathetic to Ishaq in their reporting, noting, for example, how the Harper government employed Lyndon Crosby as their campaign strategist, who is known for concocting divisive wedge issues that trade in fear and xenophobia. Other media narratives in support of Ishaq focused on the small number of women that this policy impacts each year, thus downplaying its insignificance as a relevant issue worthy of concern (Wu 2015). In another article from *Vice News*, Zakira Jogiat, who was one of the last women to be sworn in wearing a niqab prior to the 2011 restriction, spoke of being forced to "choose between my religious obligations [or] choices and my identity as a Canadian" (Nasser 2015).

Such sympathetic narratives were common in the press and mainly framed the debate around the question of religious freedom. In another article, 600 academics published an open letter in the *Ottawa Citizen* condemning the "inflammatory rhetoric of 'barbaric cultural practices'" and concluded by stating that "Toleration does not require that one like or endorse the cultural or religious practices of others, but it does require that we refrain from insulting the dignity of those with whom we disagree.[11] The Conservatives have shown contempt for a politics of mutual respect" (IDC 2015).

In these examples, we find a range of narratives that both reproduce well-worn tropes surrounding Muslim women, including reactionary stereotypes that are used to justify restrictions, as well as arguments in support of the niqab that revolve around questions of choice and religious freedom. In many cases, opposition was expressed toward the Harper government and its divisive framing of this issue and not in defense of Ishaq or niqabis *per se*. Despite Zunera Ishaq's unique public performance in defense of herself, the narrative remained much the same.

The niqab: a permanent counterpublic?

In his book *Publics and Counterpublics* (2002), Michael Warner defines a 'public' as "a kind of social totality" that "is thought to include everyone within the field in question" (65). In the broadest sense, to be part of a public "requires at least minimal participation" where the act of "[m] erely paying attention can be enough to make you a member" (71). At the same time, publics are always "mediated by cultural forms," as seen with polling data, which means that they "do not exist apart from the discourse that addresses them" (72). In other words, when considering who or what constitutes a public, basic metrics like citizenship or participation are not enough since individuals and groups of people must fall into a pattern of behavior that is recognizable, replicable, and eventually integrated as an accepted part of the body politic. All of this requires an "arbitrary social closure to contain its potentially infinite extension" where certain publics that fall outside of acceptable boundaries get classified as "personal, private or particular" (117).

In his analysis, Warner draws on Nancy Fraser's term 'subaltern counterpublics' to describe subordinate groups that "have no arenas of deliberation among themselves about their needs, objectives and strategies." Fraser goes on to describe these counterpublics as "parallel discursive arenas where members of subordinated social groups invent and circulate counterdiscourses to formulate oppositional interpretations of their identities, interests, and needs" (qtd. in Warner 118). While it appears that hijab-wearing women are developing the contours of a recognizable public, as Kassam and Mustafa point out (2017), niqabis remain outside these boundaries as a specter that points to the limitations of what secular, multicultural ideologies are able to interpret in anything but the most generalizing ways. My aim here is neither to reject nor support the niqab (e.g., on ethical or legal grounds), but rather to point out how it is primarily constructed through a combination of Orientalist imagery and secular ideology (particularly of the 'Judeo-Christian' variety), which structures its meaning and interpretation in particular ways.

In her study on veiling practices in Finland, Anne Mari Almila (2017) considers the question of space as an underexplored factor in these debates, asking, "what kind of adaptations are needed when a 'foreign' dress practice, following 'foreign' spatial logic, is brought into a different environment" (231). By 'spatial logic,' Almila is referring to the relationship between social norms in a particular society and the kind of expectations that go along with it. For example, whereas some spaces allow for public nudity in Germany, such as saunas or sections of parks, others do not and operate by different logics that would render a lack of clothing an offense. Although Almila's study is focused on 'adaptation strategies' of Muslim women in

Helsinki, especially examples of niqabis modifying and relaxing their habits in certain spaces like children's playgrounds, the same question could be posed toward non-Muslims living in Euro-Western spaces.

For example, I live in an area of Bonn, Germany, called Bad Godesberg, which has a sizable Muslim population, especially from countries such as Syria and Saudi Arabia. Many Saudi's live in Bad Godesberg on a temporary basis seeking medical treatment, with a noticeable percentage of Saudi women who wear a niqab (e.g., while shopping or walking with their children in the park). Although Germany does not have many restrictions on niqabs, in the case Bad Godesberg local demographics and economic factors contribute to a higher level of adaptation to the niqab in this area, especially when compared to different locales throughout Germany where it is rarely seen and not tied to the financial interests of the community.

By contrast, veiling controversies that gain media attention take the niqab out of spaces where partial adaptation may have occurred into a broad, open–ended terrain where people with no experience interacting with niqabis are able to project a wide range of meanings onto it, including fear and revulsion. This dynamic was very much on display in the case of Zunera Ishaq, though her numerous public appearances and attempts to assert her agency complicate the idea of the faceless, voiceless oppressed woman and provide an opportunity to ask, can there ever be a niqabi public?

The first details one comes across on Ishaq's Wikipedia page are that she came from a moderate Muslim family, that neither her father nor her husband asked her to wear the niqab (she chose to wear it at 15), and that she obtained a Master's degree in English literature while living in Pakistan. Ishaq is portrayed as a feminist fighting for gender equality who identifies with Ophelia from Shakespeare's *Hamlet*: "I found that women in English literature were also treated very harshly. . . . It's not only in Islam that people talk about women like this. I am going to fight on for the right to wear the veil. I am 90 per cent certain I will win and if I don't, I will also appeal" (Wikipedia 2020). This narrative presents a much different picture of a niqab-wearing woman than most mainstream discourse would suggest, though these details of her life were not the primary focus in Ishaq's own narratives in media interviews throughout 2015.

For the most part, Ishaq relied upon the familiar and publicly recognized discourse of religious freedom when speaking to media, while only occasionally making mention of her theological commitments. For example, in an interview on Canada's national broadcaster, the CBC, Ishaq stated that for her the niqab was a personal choice and a response to her sense of religious duty, while also stressing that it was not a requirement in her native Pakistan (CBC Radio 2015). In a similar vein, she contested the idea that she was coerced into wearing the niqab by stating, "This was not something my husband asked for, as journalists now think – I didn't know my husband at the time. My sisters made the same decision. No one compelled them to wear the veil. They just felt more comfortable" (Fisk 2015).

In another interview, Ishaq attempted to normalize herself by highlighting her career ambitions and social work, noting how she was trying to become a teacher in Canada, as she had been in Pakistan, and that she took pains to immerse herself in Canadian culture, helping to "organize a children's festival, tak[ing] part in tree-planting events and help[ing] raise funds for a women's shelter." In an effort to offset the image of the 'foreigner,' Ishaq also remarked, "If you are here you have to do something [for] the community you are living in. . . . I think all these things should be enough to prove that I'm not someone who is a stranger here" (Quan 2015).

It is hard to measure to what extent Ishaq's public performances and defiance of certain stereotypes may have contributed to support for her case, though if public opinion polls are to be trusted it appears that a majority of Canadians were very much opposed to the niqab, in general, and not just to its presence during citizenship ceremonies. As one report from the Angus Reid Institute noted, "In contrast to the majority of Canadians who support woman wearing the Hijab and a Nun's Habit – 73 per cent and 88 per cent, respectively – seven out of ten (73%) oppose Muslim women wearing a Niqab in public – a veil that covers the face, showing only the eyes" (Angus Reid 2014). Despite Ishaq's ultimate victory in the Federal Court, it would appear that her media appearances did little to sway public opinion in any discernable way.

One thing that can be said with some confidence is that the ongoing effects of Orientalist imagery continue to have a significant impact on public discourses featuring Muslims and Muslim women, especially when it comes to the niqab. It could also be argued that growing normalization of the hijab in some spaces (especially those that follow a 'Judeo-Christian' mode of secularism) is partly influenced by high-profile battles over the niqab like Ishaq's, where certain commentators will rhetorically position it in relation to the less threatening headscarf, which does not fall under the same set of concerns, such as security, intimidation, politeness, blocking communication, identification issues, and an affront to secular societies (Bakht 2009).

At the same time, there was no discernable reflection throughout the niqab affair on what veiling or other Islamic practices might mean for Muslims, and how choice might be understood differently in other cultural settings. For example, in her reflections on the Danish Cartoons affair from 2005, Saba Mahmood (2013) argues that what was absent from Western media analysis was any sort of engagement with how Islamic practices are understood by insiders, such as the common understanding of a "relation of similitude" (70) with the Prophet Muhammad, where Muslims are "encouraged to emulate how he dresses . . . how he spoke to his friends and adversaries . . . and so on" (69). The absence of any kind of engagement with these types of narratives speaks to the limitations of the concepts of choice and religious freedom as effective modes for interpreting culture in a neutral fashion. Indeed, it could be argued that by framing the secular in terms of abstract concepts such as choice, religious freedom, or multiculturalism, these terms become political footballs available to those who can make them work best.

The niqab affair was by no means a decisive variable in the defeat of Stephen Harper's Conservative party in October 2015. His use of this wedge issue was strategically effective in a narrow sense since it paired the niqab, a symbol of conservative and, to some, extremist Islam, with a central ritual of citizenship that symbolizes national identity and shared values. The foreignness of the niqab and its associations with political Islam (e.g., invoking prior fears about 'sharia law' in Canada) created a narrow enough proposition for many to endorse, at least on the surface. At the same time, by invoking gender equality as the primary reason for banning the niqab from oath-taking ceremonies, the Harper government left itself open to attack about its own record on women's issues (Kingston 2015). In this sense, the niqab served as a way for competing groups to fight a proxy war, where this symbol stood in for a broader set of issues that could be waged in its name.

One example of this proxy war was seen with the hashtag #DressCodePM, which started trending in March 2015 as a number of people from around the country framed their opposition to the Harper government's ban as an infringement on women's (and even men's) sartorial choices. For example, journalist Shireen Ahmed tweeted a photo of herself in a headscarf and a Montreal Canadians hockey jersey, writing: "@pmharper My outfit OK? Am I still part of the Canadian family?" Another woman tweeted, "I'm thinking of wearing white shoes before May 24. Is that still considered tacky? #dresscodePM," while one man chimed in, "my toque is covering my ears. is that allowed? #dresscodePM." The primary message here, as stated by Amira Elghawaby of the National Council of Canadian Muslims, is that it "is anti-women for the state or anyone at all to be telling women what they can or cannot wear" (Puzic 2015).

Although media narratives like these seemed to reflect overwhelming opposition to the ban on the basis of a liberal, multicultural conception of choice, a glance at the comments section in this same article reveals near-total opposition to the niqab. A few examples include:

> Personally, I am glad that PM Harper had the guts to say what so many of us Canadians have been thinking and feeling for many years. The pendulum has swung so far in favor of incoming cultures of immigrants

> that our own culture and norms are being bluntly ignored. . . . Justin Trudeau and Tom Mulcair [then leader of the left-leaning NDP party] are just plain embarrassing and if either one were in power our culture . . . would be pushed aside. Not only that, they would not protect us from terrorist activity NOR aid in the fight to stop these barbarians.
>
> There are dress codes everywhere so I don't think it's too much to ask a woman to remove at certain ceremonies or for identification.
>
> This is not infringing on anyone's religious beliefs but is a (or should be) requirement to become a citizen of Canada.
>
> The vast majority of the country is behind you Mister Harper. Please don't back down!
>
> (Puzic 2015)

While at least one of these comments resembles the kind of xenophobic rhetoric that is familiar in the long history of Orientalist representations, it is evident that for others the ban appeared as a reasonable limit on what states like Canada should permit. One question worth considering here is how we can account for the gap between what we might call liberal establishment sentiment and general public opinion? In one sense, by framing the issue in terms of gender equality, the Harper government was tapping into well-worn civilizational rhetoric regarding the status of women under 'Islam.' Part of the wager that the Conservatives made in deploying this wedge strategy was that liberal counter-narratives would not be able to defend the niqab on the grounds of equality and thus be painted into a corner. By framing the issue in terms of religious freedom, however, while also pointing to the "play on people's fears . . . directly toward the Muslim faith" (Wherry 2015), Trudeau was able to make use of an inclusive variety of 'Judeo-Christian' secularism that inevitably won the day. However, had the political winds not been blowing against the nearly ten-year reign of the Harper government, it is not clear that the niqab ban would have been lifted at all. Here the case of Québec offers a useful comparison.

Case study: secularism in Québec, also known as laïcité

> People can call police if secular dress code not adhered to, Québec Public Security Minister says (Boissint 2019).

So reads a *Globe and Mail* headline from April 2, 2019, on Québec's then-proposed Bill 21 to ban the wearing of religious symbols in the public sector. A quick Google search from early February 2020 yields a variety of hits on this topic from American, British, and Canadian sites, with headlines representing a range of positions. Those expressing opposition bear headlines such as "How a Quebec law banning religious symbols derails women's careers" (Guardian); "Quebec's ban causes 'irreparable harm,' teachers tell court" (CBC); and "Canada's political leaders agree Quebec's religious symbols ban is discriminatory: They also agree to do nothing about it" (*The Washington Post*). More neutral or descriptive statements appear in the following headlines: "Quebec bans religious symbols for state workers in new law" (*Global News*); "Quebec passes religious symbols secularism bill" (BBC); and "Quebec's religious symbols ban a major issue in federal election campaign" (*Globe and Mail*). It is also worth noting that one has to go the second page of Google's search engine and the fourteenth entry to find a local article from the *Montreal Gazette* that reads, "Confusion reigns as Québec schools apply religious symbols ban."

A few things can be gleaned from this small sample of an English-language Google algorithm. For one thing, there has been a considerable amount of attention outside of Québec, in the rest of Canada, and internationally to the most recent initiative of the provincial Coalition Avenir Québec Party (CAQ) to ban the wearing of religious symbols in the public sector. In one sense this attention is not surprising since, as a byline from *The Atlantic* in July 2019 puts it, "Last month, [Québec] became the first place in North America to institute such a ban." This brief and non-representative sample of Anglo-American media narratives reflects an overwhelming opposition to Bill 21 from commentators outside of Québec, where the culture and history of the province are not well understood. Here I would like to suggest that a more interesting question is what these responses reveal about contradictions inherent in the politics of secular multiculturalism?

Taken together, these articles do get the basic elements of Bill 21 correct, such as the general prohibition on wearing religious symbols (e.g., hijabs, niqabs, Sikh turbans, Jewish kippahs, and large crosses) when working in professions such as policing, law, and teaching, while bus drivers, doctors, and social workers must only keep their faces uncovered. One article from Canada's *Global News* also points out that Québec premier Francois Legault offered a compromise by allowing daycare workers and private school teachers to be exempt from the bill, along with professionals who were hired before the law took effect. Also noted are divisions within Québec's provincial political parties, with the Parti Québécois voting in favor of the bill, while the Liberals and Québec Solidaire (a small leftist party) opposed it. One of the pieces took note of the pre-emptive use of Section 33 of the Canadian Charter, the "notwithstanding clause," which allows provinces to override the Charter for a period of five years, while *The Washington Post* noted how federal leaders in Canada were reluctant to challenge Legault in the lead-up to the election in October 2019, to which he responded with glee, noting that they ought to 'stay out' of any legal challenges 'forever.'

Another common narrative contrasted federal politicians' unwillingness to stand up to discrimination to civil society groups who are working to oppose this legislation. In addition, opposition to Bill 21 from several provincial leaders in British Columbia, Alberta, Manitoba, and Ontario was also addressed – some of whom have used this opportunity to declare that they would welcome anyone who feels discriminated against to come and work in their provinces. Overall, these narratives tended to frame the issue as one of an intolerant Québec versus a more liberal and multicultural Canada, reinforced by several references to Québec's 'centre-right' government in international media, thus affectively linking this bill with the global upsurge in right-wing populism, while overlooking earlier Liberal and Parti Québécois support for similar proposals, such as Bill 60. While there are clear elements of what I have been calling Western fragility in Québec's response to the religious symbols question, representing this issue along a left/right axis fails to account for the complexities of Québec's particular nationalist identity, its adoption of French-style secularism (laïcité), and how this issue functions as a culture war in an age of ongoing neoliberal politics.

Here I would suggest that part of what has guided the negative reaction to Bill 21 outside of Québec is not merely an opposition to anti-Muslim and anti-immigrant sentiment (which is, of course, part of it), but rather the visceral response such a ban provokes against certain taken for granted ideals of 'Judeo-Christian' secularism, such as freedom of expression and religious freedom. Such ideals, as I have argued throughout this chapter, are steeped in a secular-Protestant understanding of religion and are thus ill-equipped to deal with the claims of multiple cultures. Whereas things like the climate crisis and the seemingly endless tailspin of neoliberal capitalism present larger and incalculable threats to the 'system' writ large, the very idea that certain core principles of the secular liberal project could be overturned so easily is perhaps a greater shock precisely because it represents a threat to something that many assumed was under control. In this sense, it could be argued that the response to Bill 21 is more about a crisis in Euro-Western political culture and a clash of secularisms (Judeo-Christian and laïcité) than a dispute over religious symbols *per se*. In order to make this case, I will first need to sketch out some of the main contours of Québec nationalism to better explain why religious symbols have become such a lightning-rod in these debates.

Québec nationalism, the quiet revolution, and the birth of separatism

A comprehensive analysis of Québec nationalism would have to account for, at a minimum, key events like the founding/colonization of New France, the Battle of the Plains of Abraham (1759), and the history Lower Canada

(1791–1840), all formative markers of contemporary Québécois identity. Although space does not allow for such considerations, it is important to note that after New France was taken over by England in 1763, the Catholic Church began to play an increased role in the Québec colony, taking charge of social welfare services, health, and education (Dumont 1986), thus establishing itself as a central force in the region (Zubryscki 2016).[12]

From 1900 to 1930, the Catholic Church in Québec undertook a number of initiatives in response to rapid industrialization and the 'modernizing' trends that followed. As David Seljak (1996) observes,

> Besides multiplying its institutions which provided education, health care, and social services, the Church promoted the growth of Catholic labour unions, farmers' cooperatives, credit unions, pious leagues, newspapers, radio and television shows, films, and Catholic Action groups for workers, students, women, farmers, and nationalists.
>
> (1996: 112)

As changes in the post-World War II period brought about a new coterie of university-trained bureaucrats, the Church's hold on the social fabric began to slip. After the election of Liberal Party Leader Jean Lesage in 1960, the secularization of schools, hospitals, and social services quickly followed, accompanied by the nationalization of corporations like Hydro-Québec. In addition, labor reforms and social welfare programs shifted the balance of power away from the Church toward the growing public sector, while the influence of business interests outside of the province wanned and, along with it, dependence on the English language (Seljak 1996). Accompanying these structural changes came a new 'nationalist' narrative embodied in the phrase 'L'état du Québec (the state of Québec) and the adoption of the term 'Québécois.' This is what became known as the Quiet Revolution.

I would be remiss if I did not mention the creation of the Parti Québécois in 1968 under René Lévesque, which put forward a separatist mandate. Lévesque leaned into this burgeoning Québécois identity and was elected premier in 1976, passing Bill 101 the following year, which made French Québec's official language. Alas, there is no space to detail the effects of the 1987 Meech Lake Accord and the 1992 Charlottetown Accord – both failed attempts by the federal government to make accommodations to Québec under the revised Canadian Charter of 1982. The growth of Québec separatism and failed attempts at appeasement by the Canadian state culminated in a national referendum in 1995, which lost by a hair's breadth (50.58% voted NO[N]). Both the Charlottetown Accord and the 1995 referendum are widely considered to be responses to the Canadian Multiculturalism Act of 1988, which the Québec government rejected, particularly the idea that multiculturalism must operate within a framework that is bilingual. "As an alternative," writes Meena Sharify-Funk and Elysia Guzik (2017), "Quebec developed a model of 'cultural convergence' over the 1980s and formalized its interculturalism policy in 1991," which "sets up the expectation that immigrants adopt French as their primary language . . . and that they engage in an exchange between their supposedly preserved ethnic and linguistic identities and Quebec's constantly evolving culture" (192).

Two additional variables are important to note here, including the growing influence of feminism in the 1960s and, starting in the 1970s, demographic shifts in Québec through immigration. Rising feminist sentiments in the province were very much tied to the nationalist project of women's emancipation from the patriarchal structures of the Church, embodied in the slogan "No Women's Liberation without a Free Québec, no Free Québec without women's Liberation" (qtd. in Zubrzycki, loc. 224). This sentiment continues to be reflected in opposition to Islamic veiling practices to this day. Genevieve Zubrzycki also observes that one of the unintended consequences of the Quiet Revolution was a decline in birth rates and a subsequent rise in Francophone immigration from North and West Africa, which was predominantly Muslim, thus contributing to a re-examination of the meaning of Québécois and 'Catho-laïcité.'[13] Indeed, according to the *Statistics Canada* 2001 Census, the Muslim population in Montreal doubled between 1991 and 2001 and grew to over 100,000 by 2010.

The growth of Québécois identity throughout the 1960s bolstered the use of the French language, limited the role of the Catholic Church, and lead to a new nationalist narrative championed by the Parti Québécois. Although attempts by the Canadian state to appease Québec throughout the 1980s and 1990s contributed to separatist sentiments, the failure to win an independent state in 1995 led to new strategies to shore up Québécois identity. As immigration from French-speaking countries increased the number of non-European and Muslim members of Québec society, questions of cultural heritage and identity became an increasingly important battle ground upon which provincial parties differentiated themselves from each other, and from the rest of Canada. One of the central pillars in this battleground was a homegrown variety of Catho-laïcité.

Québec and the veil

The Hérouxville Code, named after a small town of around 1300 in central Québec, made international headlines after passing a "values test" into law in 2007, with provisions such as "no stoning women in public" and "no female circumcision," clearly signaling an anti-Muslim sentiment

(Zine 2009). While there were no Muslim residents in Hérouxville at the time, waves of migration to Québec from French-speaking countries such as Algeria and Morocco throughout the 1990s contributed to fears of a looming clash of civilizations.

The controversy that followed in the wake of the Hérouxville affair prompted then-premier Jean Charest to launch the Bouchard-Taylor Commission (2007–2008) to address questions concerning "reasonable accommodation" of cultural/religious practices within Québec.[14] Underpinning the Commission's findings was a commitment to maintain two core values of Québécois society: gender equality and state neutrality. In addition, the Commission used the term 'laïcité ouverte' or 'open secularism' to signal a pluralistic model of neutrality that is not anti-religious, and a commitment to accommodate practices that fall outside of accepted norms.

One enduring problem, however, is that most accommodation requests never gain media attention, including those classified as "concerted adjustments" that occur between an employer and an employee. Instead, most of the high-profile cases tend to feature Muslims, Sikhs, and Orthodox Jews, despite the fact that "a significant number of requests for accommodation are also made by practicing Catholics, Jehovah's Witnesses, and Seventh Day Adventists" (Zubrzycki 2016: Loc. 2275). In this way, culturally dominant groups in Québec have an advantage in such matters since their requests often fly under the radar of public scrutiny, while minority groups (particularly Muslim women) face a much greater possibility that their requests will become weaponized in the culture wars.[15]

In March of 2010, the Québec Liberal Party proposed Bill 94, which required women to unveil their faces when working in the public sector or when receiving public services. The bill ultimately failed to pass.[16] In the years that followed, several other bills were proposed, including Bill 60 (September 2013), Bill 62 (October 2017), and Bill 21(March 2019). Whereas Bill 94 proposed a soft, selective restrictions targeting niqab-wearing women, Bill 60, also known as the Charter of Secular Values, attempted to ban all "conspicuous religious symbols" from being worn by employees in the public service. After Bill 60 failed to pass, the next attempt, Bill 62, followed a pattern of restrictions reminiscent of Bill 94, by prohibiting niqab-wearers from receiving public services, including the use of public transport. This prompted protests on buses in Montreal, where opponents of the bill wore surgical masks, scarves, and other face coverings in solidarity with niqabis, who, as one person puts it, would limit "their access to services that should be a fundamental right for all Quebecers" (Henry & Kestler-D'Amours 2019). Bill 62 was eventually suspended as a possible violation of the Canadian Charter of Rights and Freedoms and remained in limbo until the Liberals were defeated in October 2018. Bill 21, titled "An act respecting the laicity of the state," returned to the broader ban on all religious symbols for public employees, while doubling down on face-veil bans when accessing public services, including public transport.

When considering the various changes to these bills over the course of a decade, it is hard to overlook the targeting of Muslim women and how pushback against Bills 94, 60, and 62 contributed to changes in the official justification for the proposed restrictions – from championing women's equality to a broader idea of state neutrality. For example, whereas recommendations by the government sponsored Conseil du statut de la femme (CSF) Report on Bill 94 from 2011 "strongly critiques Canadian multiculturalism as threatening this laïque vision of gender equality" and "argues that the rights of women are denied by multicultural protections" (Selby 2014: 449), Bill 60 and Bill 21 focus on restricting all 'religious symbols.'

As with the case of Reus, Spain in 2010, public concerns over targeting Muslim women led to proposals for broader restrictions so as to avoid the appearance of prejudice, thus shifting the primary justification from gender equality to the neutrality of the state. Although Muslim women and other minority groups, such as turban-wearing Sikh men, are still disproportionality targeted under these wider restrictions, a case could be made that the current construction of the secular in Québec has more to do with intercultural political maneuvering and the relationship to the Canadian state than it does to any stable notion of secular values.

Bill 60: the charter of (secular) values

Back in December of 2013, I attended an event at the provincial legislature in Winnipeg, Manitoba, titled "Day Affirming Human Rights and Religious Diversity for All Canadians: Non! To the Québec Charter of Values." The event was one of several across the country in opposition to Bill 60 and reflected a common sentiment outside of Québec – namely, that the proposed bill was in violation of The Canadian Charter of Rights and Freedoms and threatened to stoke racism and undermine religious diversity and religious freedom.

In a blog post that I wrote about this event at the time, I made note of the clear impact that the proposal had had on Muslim women, citing reports of a 300 per cent increase in anti-Muslim attacks by the Québec Collective Against Islamophobia. I also observed that the proposed bill was opposed by the leaders of all federal political parties in Canada and that it would, therefore, be easily defeated if brought before the Supreme Court. One obvious angle to my mind, both then as now, was that the Parti Québécois was hoping for such a legal challenge as it would allow them to claim that Canada was violating Québec's sovereignty and thus bolster their popularity in the province (Sheedy 2013). As previously noted, one reason for Bill 60's ultimate demise was that it highlighted the difficulty of proposing a broad religious symbols ban, since it was perceived as an attack on all (or most) religions, thus rousing a larger constituency in opposition to it. For most of the commentators outside of Québec, Bill 60 was perceived as a threat to Canadian multiculturalism and hence to one version of 'Judeo-Christian' secularism.

When Bill 21 was proposed in 2019, a majority of Canadian and international commentators interpreted the Coalition Avenir Québec's plans as a symptom of growing ethno-nationalism as discussed at the outset of this section. What was largely missed in most of this commentary was threefold: first, an examination of how religious symbols function as a type of culture war that has come to replace separatism in the struggle for Québec sovereignty; second, a reckoning with the basic dynamics of party politics in the province, including the role of civil society groups; and third, a reckoning with how the legacies of the Quiet Revolution have contributed to Québec's particular brand of Catho-laïcité. Taken together, the Québec case is a prime example of the use of the secular as a tool of state power, where questions of equality and neutrality are ultimately subordinate to the larger goal of managing difference.

One example that highlights these overlooked narratives can be seen in official meetings between political parties and civil society groups over Bill 60 back in 2013. As Emily Laxer (2019) observes, Québec's main political parties drew upon competing visions of nationhood during these debates in hopes of gaining an electoral advantage over their competitors. As she writes:

> Utilized by the Parti Québécois leadership, the discourse of "courage" portrayed the Charter of Values as a brave and audacious step in disentangling Quebec from the legal and political limitations imposed by Canadian federalism. A second discourse – that of "responsibility" – was used by the Parti libéral du Québec to emphasize discontinuities between the Charter and the universal rights and freedoms that designate belonging in a "modern" society. A third discourse, which I call nationalism's "third way," captures the dilemmas that the Charter posed for factions within the sovereignty movement that see immigrant inclusion as crucial to an independent Quebec.
>
> (156)

One thing to note here is the framing of this issue as a matter of values versus rights. With reference to secularism, gender equality, and the French language, the PQ framed national belonging in terms of having the 'courage' to uphold Québec values rather than Canadian legal rights. For the Liberals who opposed the bill, the "responsible" path meant finding a balance between "respect for the neutrality of the state, gender equality, and Quebec's heritage" (Laxer: 179). As for the "third way," the Charter of Values opened up a divide in the province's sovereignty movement between those who view universal rights for immigrants as essential for achieving Québec's independence and those who use cultural and linguistic differences as a wedge issue to gain support from more traditional Francophone voters. These tensions between linguistic and cultural sovereignty, Québec heritage, and universal rights can also be seen in briefs from civil society groups who participated in public hearings on Bill 60. As Laxer writes:

> Slightly less than half (45 per cent) of the briefs approved this ban, whereas 49 per cent opposed it and nearly 6 per cent did not state any clear opinion on the matter. Support for the ban was most prominent among *concerned citizens, along with representatives of pro-secularism, feminist, and atheist/humanist organizations, whereas the lowest support rates were among representatives of religious groups, university/school board, teachers, and labour market organizations, as well as organizations representing service providers* [my emphasis]. (159)

For several pro-Charter groups, the Quiet Revolution was used to mark a difference between backwardness and modernity, with some even invoking this history to depict "immigrant religious signs" as "intentional efforts" to betray this legacy (161). This included some feminist groups who, according to one critic, "have projected their anger with the Catholic Church onto Muslim women," thus equating gender inequality in the Catholic Church with Islam writ large (163). Others in the anti-Charter camp expressed a different view of the secular legacy of the Quiet Revolution, stressing the value of pluralism and the idea that "Québec must learn to incorporate the minorities within its territory." Related to this was a concern with how such a ban would be viewed on the world stage and what damage it might do to Québec's reputation as a "modern state of law" (164).

Whereas pro-Charter feminist groups rejected multiculturalism as a barrier to achieving universal feminism, and drew links between Canadian multiculturalism and Québec's history of colonial rule under the British, newer feminist organizations took a different tack. For example, the creation of the Collective des féministes musulmanes du Québec (Collective of Muslim Feminists of Quebec, CFMQ) during this time brought a younger, more diverse and "intersectional or postcolonial" feminism to the table, thus highlighting contrasting positions between older and younger generations, as well as divisions along ethnic and religious lines. Ultimately, the CFMQ boycotted the hearings, with one representative stating:

> We knew the process was not being conducted in good faith, that it was not actually a process of genuinely wanting to consult anybody about this Charter. It was really more about the government being able to say, 'Hey, look, we had a consultation process and we talked to people.' It was a way of giving them legitimacy in what they were trying to do. We didn't want to be part of that.
>
> (qtd. in Laxer: 169)

This feeling of distrust among the (then) newly formed Collective of Muslim Feminists of Québec reflects the growing presence of active Muslim women entering into the political sphere and challenging prevailing orthodoxies. At the same time, their failure to persuade decision makers also reflects the still marginal position of Muslim groups in Québec and their inability to shape public sentiments when it comes to questions of gender equality and competing interpretations of the veil. The growing presence of such groups does, however, make it hard to reduce the veil to one-dimensional representations and contributes to the logic of restricting all religious symbols as an expression of the secular.

Conclusion

In July 2019, headlines reported that the cross hanging in Québec's National Assembly since 1936 was being removed after much debate over whether it represented a religious symbol or a cultural symbol of the province's heritage (CBC News 2019). For many social theorists, including scholars of religion, this dilemma reflects an instance of reification in Georg Lukács's sense of the term, where people grant meaning to objects that are really about social relationships between people and things. In this sense, the meaning of a cross is not only both religious and cultural but also inanimate, irrelevant, and ignored depending on one's socialization and relationship to this particular object. The battle over whether the cross is cultural or religious ultimately comes down to the intersection between power and persuasion, on the one hand, and social context, on the other hand.

Before the introduction of Bill 60, there were no widespread calls to remove crosses from the National Assembly, or from the many municipal buildings in cities and towns throughout the province. Prior to this time, as Zubrzycki observes, "walking the thin line between [the] 'Catholic' and secular distinction" had been achieved "by refiguring religion as culture, heritage, and patrimony" (Loc. 2190). Although 'Catholic' symbols such as crosses have never held a universal meaning, they did not become a site of serious controversy in Québec until political and cultural forces in the province began singling out the veil as a threat to secular values. It was only after attempts to classify certain types of veiling as a threat to laïcité that the presence of crosses became increasingly suspect as a neutral symbol of "culture, heritage, and patrimony." Far from re-signifying the cross as merely 'religious' once again, the latest restrictions on certain symbols in Québec reveal the contradictions of secularism as a neutral arbiter of cultural differences. Apart from the value of many laws that some call secular, the case of Québec calls attention to the political uses of this concept as a tool of national and cultural governance that is shaped just as much by the winds of cultural conflict than any secure principles that are said to define it.

Notes

1 Evelyn Alsultany (2012: 79), Elizabeth Bucar (2012: 74), Saba Mahmood (2015: 45), and Joan Scott (2018: 20) also draw on the example of Lord Cromer in their analysis.
2 The trope of the veiled Muslim women as a suicide bomber can be found in two Academy Award winning films, *Zero Dark Thirty* (2012) and *American Sniper* (2014).
3 Here they build upon Sherene Razack's (2008) classification of the imperiled Muslim woman, the dangerous Muslim man, and the civilized European.
4 One example of this phenomenon can be seen with the Canadian online news site *Rebel Media*, which has been characterized as 'alt-right' (Perry & Scrivens 2019).
5 See Razack (2008), chapter 5.
6 For a detailed account of the sharia debate in Ontario, see Ruby (2019).
7 Elizabeth Bucar's recent book *Pious Fashion* (2020) is exemplary of this trend, where she conducts fieldwork in major cities in Iran, Turkey, and Indonesia to show how veiling relates to cultural conventions, theologies, class status, beauty standards, etc.
8 See chapter 3 in Alsultany (2012).
9 All of these examples are drawn from chapter 2 of Vakulenko's *Islamic Veiling in Legal Discourses* (2012).
10 As Vakulenko (2012) puts it, "Such candid privileging of the Christian tradition above others is possible in Germany as, unlike France, it never tried to frame itself as an ideologically secular state" (120).
11 In June 2015, the Harper government passed an Act, titled "Zero Tolerance for Barbaric Cultural Practices," focusing on polygamy, forced marriage, and childhood marriage.
12 For an historical overview of the Catholic Church's role in Québec from the seventeenth to the twenty-first century, see Zubryscki (2016), esp. chapter 1.
13 The term 'Catho-laïcité' is meant to highlight the influence of Catholicism on the development and character of laïcité, including its continued influence as a marker of historical and cultural identity.
14 For a critique of the idea of requests for accommodation, see Barras (2016).

15 Selby, Barras, and Beaman's *Beyond Accommodation: Everyday Narratives of Muslim Canadians* (2018) addresses this disparity by demonstrating how the majority of accommodation requests by Muslims in Canada are made without much fanfare, despite the common media framing of conflict or culture clash.

16 Bill 94 centered around the case of Naima Atef Ahmed, an Egyptian immigrant to Québec who contested her expulsion from government-run French classes for wearing a niqab. For an extensive analysis of Bill 94, see Selby (2014).

Works cited

Abu-Odeh, L. 1991. Post-Colonial Feminism and the Veil: Considering the Differences. *New England Law Review*, 6, pp. 1527–1537.

Ahmed, L. 1992. *Women and Gender in Islam: Historical Roots of a Modern Debate*. New Haven, CT: Yale University Press.

Ahmed, L. 2011. *A Quiet Revolution: The Veil's Resurgence, from the Middle East to America*. New Haven, CT: Yale University Press.

Ahmed, S. 2004. Affective Economies. *Social Text 79*, 22(2), pp. 117–139.

Almila, A. 2017. Veiling, Gender, and Space: On the fluidity of "Public" and "Private". In: *The Routledge International Handbook to Veils and Veiling*. New York: Routledge, pp. 231–245.

Alsultany, E. 2012. *Arabs and Muslims in the Media: Race and Representation after 9/11*. New York: New York University Press.

Angus Reid, 2014. Most Canadians view Muslim community as a partner, not a problem in the fight against radicalization. *Angus Reid Institute*, November 24. Available at: https://angusreid.org/homegrown-terrorism-radicalization-canada-overblown-serious-threat/ [Accessed 18 June 2021].

Bakht, N. 2009. Veiled Objections: Facing Public Opposition to the Niqab. In: L. Beaman, ed., *Reasonable Accommodation: Managing Religious Diversity*. Vancouver: UBC Press, pp. 70–108.

Barras, A. 2016. Exploring the Intricacies and Dissonances of Religious Governance: The Case of Quebec and the Discourse of Request. *Critical Research on Religion*, 4(1), pp. 57–71.

Boissint, J. 2019. People Can Call Police If Secular Dress Code Not Adhered to, Québec Public Security Minister Says. *The Globe & Mail*, April 3. Available at: www.theglobeandmail.com/canada/article-people-can-call-police-if-secular-dress-code-not-adhered-to-quebec/ [Accessed 20 January 2021].

Bucar, E. 2012. *The Islamic Veil: A Beginners Guide*. Oxford: Oneworld Publications.

Bucar, E. 2020. *Pious Fashion: How Muslim Women Dress*. Cambridge: Harvard University Press.

Burchardt, M., Griera, M. 2019. Secular Affect and Urban Exclusion: Feelings about Burkas in Public Spaces. In: M. Scheer, N. Fadil, B. S. Johansen, eds., *Secular Bodies, Affects, and Emotions: European Configurations*. London: Bloomsbury Academic, pp. 185–204.

CBC News. 2019. Crucifix Removed from National Assembly's Blue Room. *CBC News*, July 9. Available at: www.cbc.ca/news/canada/montreal/crucifix-removed-national-assembly-from-blue-room-1.5205352 [Accessed 20 January 2021].

CBC Radio. 2015. Why Zunera Ishaq Fought for Her Niqab and Became and Election Issue. *The Current*, October 8. Available at: www.cbc.ca/radio/the-current/the-current-for-october-8-2015-1.3262082/why-zunera-ishaq-fought-for-her-niqab-and-became-an-election-issue-1.3262092 [Accessed 20 January 2021].

Crawford, A. 2015. Justin Trudeau Drops Controversial Niqab Appeal. *CBC*, November 16. Available at: www.cbc.ca/news/politics/niqab-appeal-appeal-citizenship-ceremonies-canada-jody-wilson-raybould-1.3321264 [Accessed 20 January 2021].

Cronin, S. 2014. Introduction: Coercion or Empowerment? Anti-Veiling Campaigns: A Comparative Perspective. In: S. Cronin, ed., *Anti-Veiling Campaigns in the Muslims World: Gender, Modernism, and the Politics of Dress*. New York: Routledge, pp. 1–36.

Dumont, F. 1986. Histoire du catholicisme Québécois, historie d'une sociéte. *Recherches sociogragraphiques*, 27, pp. 115–125.

Falah, G. 2005. The Visual Representation of Muslim/Arab Women in Daily Newspapers in the United States. In: G. Falah, ed., *Geographies of Muslims Women: Gender, Religion, and Space*, eBook. New York: The Guildford Press, pp. 4308–4773.

Fernando, M. 2014. *The Republic Unsettled: Muslim French and the Contradictions of Secularism*. Durham: Duke University Press.

Fisk, R. 2015. Niqab Row: Canada's Government Challenges Ruling Zunera Ishaq Can Wear Veil While Taking Oath of Citizenship. *The Independent*, September 30. Available at: www.independent.co.uk/news/world/americas/niqab-row-canada-s-government-challenges-ruling-zunera-ishaq-can-wear-veil-while-taking-oath-citizenship-a6674151.html [Accessed 20 January 2021].

Haddad, Y. 2007. The Post-9/11 *Hijab* as Icon. *Sociology of Religion*, 68(3), pp. 253–267.

Haddad, Y., Smith, J., Moore, M. 2006. *Muslim Women in America: The Challenge of Islamic Identity Today*. New York: Oxford University Press.

Hamandi, A. 2015. For Women, Harper's Government Has Been a Disaster. *iPolitics*, September 22. Available at: https://ipolitics.ca/2015/09/22/for-women-harpers-government-has-been-a-disaster/ (Accessed 18 June 2021].

Henry, S., Kestler-D'Amours, J. 2017. Montreal Protesters Don Surgical Masks, Scarves over New Face-Covering Law. *CBC News*, October 20. Available at: www.cbc.ca/news/canada/montreal/quebec-bill-62-religious-law-1.4363647 [Accessed 20 January 2021].

IDC. 2015. Open Letter Regarding Conservative Party Campaign Tactics. *In Due Course: A Canadian Public Affairs Blog*. Available at: http://induecourse.ca/open-letter-regarding-conservative-party-campaign-tactics/ [Accessed 20 January 2021].

Kassam, S., Mustafa, N. 2017. Veiling Narratives: Discourses of Canadian Multiculturalism, Acceptability and Citizenship. In: *The Routledge International Handbook on Veils and Veiling*. New York: Routledge, pp. 73–83.

Kay, B. 2015. Zunera Ishaq Does a Disservice to Women Forced to Wear the Veil. *National Post*, February 17. Available at: https://nationalpost.com/opinion/

barbara-kay-zunera-ishaq-does-a-disservice-to-women-forced-to-wear-the-veil [Accessed 20 January 2021].

Kestler-D'Amours, J. 2019. What's behind Québec's Ban on Religious Symbols? *The Atlantic*, July 16. Available at: www.theatlantic.com/international/archive/2019/07/quebec-bans-religious-symbols/593998/ [Accessed 20 January 2021].

Kingston, A. 2015. Why Stephen Harper Doesn't Want to Talk about Women's Issues. *McLean's*, September 11. Available at: www.macleans.ca/politics/ottawa/why-stephen-harper-doesnt-want-to-talk-about-womens-issues/ [Accessed 20 January 2021].

Kroet, C. 2016. Manuel Valls: Burkini "Not Compatible" with French Values. *Politico*, August 17. Available at: www.politico.eu/article/manuel-valls-burkini-not-compatible-with-french-values/ [Accessed 20 January 2021].

Laxer, E. 2019. *Unveiling the Nation: The Politics of Secularism in France and Quebec*. Montreal, Kingston: McGill-Queen's University Press.

Mahmood, S. 2004. *Politics of Piety: The Islamic Revival and the Feminist Subject*. Princeton, NJ: Princeton University Press.

Mahmood, S. 2006. Secularism, Hermeneutics, and Empire: The Politics of Islamic Reformation. *Public Culture*, 18(2), pp. 323–347.

Mahmood, S. 2013. Religious Reason and Secular Affect: An Incommensurable Divide? In: Asad et al., eds., *Is Critique Secular? Injury, Blasphemy, and Free Speech*. Berkeley: The Townsend Center for the Humanities, pp. 64–100.

Mahmood, S. 2015. *Religious Difference in a Secular Age: A Minority Report*. Princeton, NJ: Princeton University Press.

Massad, J. 2015. *Islam in Liberalism*. Chicago: University of Chicago Press.

McKenzie, S. 2016. London Activists, J.K. Rowling React to Burkini Ban in France. *CNN*, August 26. Available at: https://edition.cnn.com/2016/08/25/europe/burkini-ban-protest-london-french-embassy/index.html [Accessed 20 January 2021].

Nasser, S. 2015. Canadian PM Stephen Harpers Controversial Vow to Ban the Niqab during Citizenship Ceremonies. *Vice News*, March 20. Available at: www.vice.com/en/article/yvxgwg/harpers-vow-to-ban-the-niqab-during-citizenship-ceremony-a-likely-election-issue [Accessed 20 January 2021].

Okin, S. 1999. Is Multiculturalism Bad for Women? In: J. Cohen, M. Nussbaum, eds., *Is Multiculturalism Bad for Women?* Princeton, NJ: Princeton University Press.

Perry, B., Scrivens, R. 2018. *Right-Wing Extremism in Canada*, eBook. Cham, Switzerland: Palgrave MacMillan.

Puzic, S. 2015. #Dresscodepm: Twitter responses to Harper's Niqab Comment. *CTV News*, March 11. Available at: www.ctvnews.ca/politics/dresscodepm-twitter-responds-to-harper-s-niqab-comment-1.2274401 [Accessed 20 January 2021].

Quan, D. 2015. Zunera Ishaq on Why She Fought To Wear a Niqab during Citizenship Ceremony: 'A Personal Attack on Me and Muslim Women.' *National Post*, February 16. Available at: https://nationalpost.com/news/canada/zunera-ishaq-the-woman-who-fought-to-wear-a-niqab-during-her-citizenship-ceremony [Accessed 18 June 2021].

Quinn, B. 2016. French Police Make Woman Remove Clothing on Nice Beach Following Burkini Ban. *The Guardian*, August 24. Available at: www.theguardian.com/world/2016/aug/24/french-police-make-woman-remove-burkini-on-nice-beach [Accessed 20 January 2021].

Razack, S. 2008. *Casting Out: The Eviction of Muslims from Western Law and Politics*. Toronto: University of Toronto Press.

Ruby, T. 2019. *Muslim Women's Rights: Contesting Liberal-Secular Sensibilities in Canada*. New York: Routledge.

Sauer, B., Rosenberger, S. 2005. VEIL: Values, Equality and Differences in Liberal Democracies: Debates about Muslim Headscarves in Europe. *Proposal, EU, Research Arena*, 7.2.1.

Scott Wallach, J. 2007. *The Politics of the Veil*. Princeton, NJ: Princeton University Press.

Scott Wallach, J. 2018. *Sex and Secularism*. Princeton, NJ: Princeton University Press.

Selby, J. 2014. Un-Veiling Women's Bodies: Secularism and Sexuality in Full-Face Veil Prohibitions in France and Québec. *Studies in Religion/Sciences Religieuses*, 43(3), pp. 439–466.

Selby, J., Barras, A., Beaman, L. 2018. *Beyond Accommodation: Everyday Narratives of Muslim Canadians*. Vancouver: UBS Press.

Seljak, D. 1996. Why the Quiet Revolution Was "Quiet": The Catholic Church's Reaction to the Secularization of Nationalism in Québec after 1960. *CCHA Historical Studies*, 62, pp. 109–124.

Sharify-Funk, M., Guzik, E. 2017. Muslim Veiling and the Legacy of Laïcité. In: *Everyday Sacred: Religion in Contemporary Quebec*. Montreal, Kingston: McGill-Queen's University Press, pp. 186–211.

Sheedy, M. 2013. On "Religious Symbols" and the Politics of Perception. *Bulletin for the Study of Religion* [blog], December 20. Available at: https://bulletin.equinoxpub.com/2013/12/on-religious-symbols-and-the-politics-of-perception/ [Accessed 20 January 2021].

Shryock, A., ed. 2010. *Islamophobia/Islamophilia: Beyond the Politics of Enemy and Friend*. Bloomington: Indiana University Press.

Vakulenko, A. 2012. *Islamic Veiling in Legal Discourses*. New York: Routledge.

Warner, M. 2002. *Publics and Counterpublics*. New York: Zone Books.

Wherry, A. 2015. Justin Trudeau and the Niqab. *McLean's*, March 10. Available at: www.macleans.ca/politics/justin-trudeau-and-the-niqab/ [Accessed 20 January 2021].

Wherry, A. 2021. Erin O'Toole Moves to Shake Off the Trumpian Taint. CBC News, January 19. Available at: https://www.cbc.ca/news/politics/erin-otoole-conservative-party-donald-trump-1.5878211 [Accessed 8 June 2021].

Wikipedia, 2020. Zunera Ishaq. Available at: https://en.wikipedia.org/wiki/Zunera_Ishaq [Accessed 20 January 2021].

Wu, S. 2015. Dead Cat on the Canadian Campaign Trail. *Harvard Political Review*, October 18. Available at: https://harvardpolitics.com/tag/zunera-ishaq/ [Accessed 20 January 2021].

Yeğenoğlu, M. 1998. *Colonial Fantasies: Toward a Feminist Reading of Orientalism*. Cambridge: Cambridge University Press.

YouTube, 2013. The Stream – Who Speaks for Muslim Women? *Al Jazeera*. Available at: https://www.youtube.com/watch?v=KhEeDA4cllk [Accessed 18 June 2021].

Zebiri, K. 2010. Orientalist Themes in Contemporary British Islamophobia. In: J. Esposito, I., Kalin, eds., *Islamophobia: The Challenge of Pluralism in the 21st Century*. New York: Oxford University Press, pp. 173–190.

Zine, J. 2009. Unsettling the Nation: Gender, Race and Muslim Cultural Politics in Canada. *Studies in Ethnicity and Nationalism*, 9(1), pp. 146–163.

Zubrzycki, G. 2016. *Beheading the Saint: Nationalism, Religion, and Secularism in Quebec*. Chicago: University of Chicago Press.

3 Are ex-Muslims atheists?

In an episode on her podcast *Polite Conversations* from March 2018, host Eiynah (a pseudonym) laments the state of movement atheism as follows:

> I have seen so many good atheists in the past two years just remove atheist or sceptic from their social media handles, or remove it from their bios, or just step out of the scene altogether because they've had enough of it. What it's turning into is a crypto-right wing movement that insists it is liberal. . . . I can't tell you how many people write to me and say that they cringe at the term atheist, not because it means a lack of belief in God, which is all fine and good, but because of the types of representatives that we have out there are joining hands with members of the alt-right.
>
> (Polite Converstions 2018)

In an earlier episode from September 2017, Eiynah reflects on her own use of the term 'Ex-Muslim,' stating, on the one hand:

> [It was] something which was quite noble-seeming to me, even a year ago, because of the way that apostacy is perceived in the Islamic world, and how many people are oppressed and silenced just for having doubt; killed even in Muslim countries. I've lived in Saudi Arabia, I've lived in Pakistan, I know what that fear is like, and I feel like that's why using this defiant term that still has the term Muslim but puts "ex" in front of it was important. Just to normalize apostacy.

On the other hand, she also notes:

> I'm starting to have issues myself with the [Ex-Muslim] movement just because of the kinds of people I see representing it and what they are saying, and who they are aligned with. And now it has gotten to the

DOI: 10.4324/9781003031239-3

> point where, post-Charlottesville, some of the takes have been, "Islam is worse than Nazism." And respected Ex-Muslims are backing this up. I don't know what's happening anymore.
>
> (Polite Conversations 2017a)

Eiynah is among a small, but growing number of digital media personalities who have begun to differentiate themselves from 'movement atheism' on account of its affinities with culturally conservative or right-leaning ideas, especially in online spaces.[1] Among her reasons for this shift is a growing awareness that atheist and ex-Muslim identities are not synonymous with 'secular values,' such as skepticism, equality rights, and a commitment to self-critique. Eiynah's dilemma thus calls attention to the fluid nature of categories like atheist and ex-Muslim and to the difficulty of relying on shared principles or values as a measure of group identity.

In posing the question "are ex-Muslims atheists?" I will not be defending a normative definition of either of these terms. Instead, my interest lies primarily in contextualizing and historicizing such terms as fluid "acts of identification" (Bayart 2005), with particular attention to how they have developed in the post-9/11 period – first, in the work of popular authors and, second, in online spaces where both of these communities thrive.

During the mid-to-late 2000s, the ascendency of the 'New Atheism' was dominated by a rhetoric of science, reason, and 'secular liberal values,' which grew largely in response to the 9/11 attacks and the rising influence of the 'Christian Right' under the presidency of George W. Bush. Through best-selling books, news and talk show appearances, along with the growth of video-sharing platforms such as YouTube, figures like Richard Dawkins, Sam Harris, and Christopher Hitchens had an outsized influence in shaping the development of movement atheism. This was also true of figures like Ayaan Hirsi Ali, who became the first best-selling ex-Muslim author during this time period. Beginning in the 2010s, movement atheist figures began to shift their attention toward defending free speech and rejecting political correctness, which I argue was the result of two main factors – the wanning appeal of the New Atheist's scientistic worldview and a response to repeated accusations of Islamophobia.[2] As we will see, the question of Islamophobia is also a central factor in the construction of ex-Muslim identities.

In what follows, I argue that ex-Muslim identities in the Euro-West have been primarily constructed through movement atheism, which often trades in anti-Islamic rhetoric and provides a recognizable path to gain support and legitimacy. Before looking at some common assemblages of ex-Muslim identities, I will first provide an overview of the evolution of movement atheism in the post-9/11 period, followed by narratives from several writers that have informed ex-Muslim identities in the Anglo-American world.

Some common atheist assemblages

The New Atheism

The dramatic rise of movement atheism in the Anglo-American world is often attributed to the so-called New Atheist authors such as Sam Harris (2004), Richard Dawkins (2006), Daniel Dennett (2006), and Christopher Hitchens (2007) – collectively dubbed the four horsemen – all of whom wrote best-selling books against religion following the 9/11 attacks. Writing over a decade later in his preface to *The Four Horsemen: The Conversation That Sparked an Atheist Revolution* (2019), Stephen Fry remarks:

> [They had] broken new ground in the English-speaking world, opening up debate everywhere, empowering humanism and secularism for a new generation, and giving voice to the always lurking and now growing suspicion that the worst aspects of religion, from faith-healing fakery to murderous martyrdom, could not be separated from the essential nature of religion itself. . . . [Their books] appeared against a millennial background of growing Christian evangelical fundamentalism in the United States and murderous jihadism in the Islamic world.
>
> (xiv)

Fry is certainly correct that the New Atheists helped to empower atheist, secular humanist, rationalist, and freethinker movements in the post-9/11 era, including the growth of organizations, websites, conferences, periodicals, and journals (Bullivant 2020).[3] Likewise, we can see their imprint on the emergence of the census category 'Nones,' along with the growth of the academic study of secularism and nonreligion (Lee 2015). While Fry's claim that their books appeared against a growing evangelical fundamentalism in the United States is defensible,[4] the phrase "murderous jihadism in the Islamic world" reflects a tendency among New Atheist figures to center 'religion' as a primary mode of identity and separate it from the socio-historical, political, and economic contexts that give shape to its countless variations.

Looking back at the peak of the New Atheists' influence during the mid-to-late 2000s, we can see how calls to replace religion with science and reason was a central impulse in their work. This impulse can be gleaned from the title of Richard Dawkin's 2009 best-selling book, *The Greatest Show on Earth: The Evidence for Evolution*, along with Sam Harris's 2014 book *Waking Up: A Guide to Spirituality Without Religion*. Harris also tried his hand at promoting a scientific morality in his 2010 offering *The Moral Landscape: How Science Can Determine Human Values*, while Daniel

Dennett's *Breaking the Spell: Religion as a Natural Phenomenon* (2006), contributed to the genre of naturalistic ontology, seeking to replace supernatural reasoning with theories of evolution and neuroscience as viable alternatives.

While it is hard to measure the extent to which these narratives have contributed to combating bad science (e.g., creationism), part of the early success of the New Atheists can be attributed to their Western-centric rhetoric – what Stephen Bullivant (2010) refers to as "patriotism atheism" (120). This rhetoric helped to replace Cold War associations between atheism and 'godless communism' with an image that was more palatable to mainstream ideology – namely, by linking atheism to establishment critiques of Islam at the height of the so-called war on terror (YouTube 2011).

As the New Atheists popularity rose, so too did criticism of Harris and Hitchens for their support of the Iraq war, while charges of Islamophobia were soon to follow (Dickson 2010). This critique also dogged fellow travelers Bill Maher (Sloan & Savage 2017) and ex-Muslim Ayaan Hirsi Ali, whose polemics against Islam and unflinching defense of a Western-centric worldview contributed to narratives that would come characterize the new culture wars in the age of social media. In addition to their preoccupation with Islam, other common themes found among New Atheists include a general adherence to neoliberal ideology (Johnson & Shirazi 2019), and a distaste for critical and cultural theories, especially when it comes to questions of race, gender, and sexual identity (Nagle 2017). As Stephen LeDrew (2016) observes:

> The New Atheism and the secular movement are too diverse to simply label them liberal or conservative, but a connection to the right wing of the political spectrum emerges in several key areas: security (particularly in terms of the West's relationship with the Muslim world and the role of the state), economics, and gender.
>
> (178)

Riding on the coattails of the New Atheist wave, academics such as Jerry Coyne, Michael Shermer, and Lawrence Krauss published books on the virtues of atheism, while promoting scientific alternatives to religion, such as Darwinian evolution and physics. LeDrew (2016) refers to these thinkers as the 'second wave' of New Atheists, which also includes A.C. Grayling, P.Z. Myers, Victor Stenger, Steven Pinker, and Ayaan Hirsi Ali. To this list we could also add Neil DeGrasse Tyson, who was the host of a 2014 remake of Carl Sagan's *Cosmos* series. Less commonly acknowledged in these circles are strands of feminist (Gaylor 1997), queer (Beredjick 2017), and non-white atheisms, such as 'Black freethinkers' (Cameron 2019), which tend to center critiques of patriarchal, hetero-normative, and racial hierarchies in Christian cultures.

Asking why these assemblages have not been integrated into popular atheism is an important question to consider as it speaks to the (often unspoken) ideological and political aims of these movements and how the influence of more prominent figures, such as Dawkins and Harris, have had a disproportionate impact on the public face of movement atheism. It is also worth asking to what extent "humanism and secularism," as Fry notes earlier, are significant variables of movement atheism today?

As I will argue later, appeals to science, reason, and secularism don't appear to be central markers of atheism beyond certain intellectual circles. Part of this can be attributed to the mainstreaming of nonreligious identities as more people come "out of the closet" and assert their cultural power (Cimino & Smith 2011). In addition, the enduring appeal of Western civilizational rhetoric and the surge of identity-based politics following the election of Donald Trump has opened up space for broader alliances between atheists and non-atheists, especially among those who profess an opposition to multiculturalism and political correctness.[5]

The politics of old and New Atheisms

Early critiques of New Atheism tended to come from theologians defending "the case for religion" (Haught 2008; McGrath 2007), with the notable exception of Chris Hedges' *When Atheism Becomes Religion* (2009) and Terry Eagleton's *Reason, Faith, and Revolution* (2010) – both of which elide the familiar 'religion versus science' framing in favor of a political analysis of this phenomenon. While often insightful, these latter texts do not consider the broader cultural reception of these ideas within Euro-Western societies.[6] Academic responses were soon to follow, such as Amarnath Amarasingam's edited volume *Religion and the New Atheism* (2010), which featured scholarly analysis from the fields of religious studies, the sociology of religion, cognitive science, philosophy, and theology. Importantly, the sociological contributions in this volume compared the New Atheists to other atheist, humanist, and secular movements, thus historicizing their influence beyond present-day concerns.

Building on this research, Richard Cimino and Christopher Smith (2014) argue that whereas skeptic organizations like the Center for Inquiry (c. 1991) had previously focused their efforts on legal battles in support of church-state separation, and have often aligned with religious groups in their efforts, newer atheist formations are "primarily interested in cultural change and attempting to construct secularist and atheist alternatives at all levels of the existing social order" (104). This shift in strategy toward gaining cultural recognition is indicative of the growing power of such communities, as witnessed by the widely attended 2012 Reason Rally in Washington DC, and the 2008–2009 Atheist Bus Campaign (Bullivant & Tomlins 2016).

Stephen LeDrew's *The Evolution of Atheism* (2016) offers an important contribution to this literature by exploring the politics of the New Atheism in relation to the broader "secular movement" that preceded it. One of his central aims, which I build upon in this chapter, is to contest the idea that "the secular movement is liberal and progressive" by showing how "it contains a deeply conservative dimension" (2–3).[7] Drawing on intra-atheist debates beginning in the mid-nineteenth century, LeDrew distinguishes between what he calls *scientific* and *humanistic* atheism.

Those who adhered to scientific atheism, such as Auguste Comte, Herbert Spencer, and EB Tylor, tended to promote some version of Darwinism and sought to understand the origins of human societies in naturalistic terms. These "Victorian Darwinists" LeDrew writes, adhered to an "explanatory model of religion, as well as political liberalism and a defense of the Enlightenment principles of progress, universalism, and scientific-rationalism" (24). For these thinkers, religion was understood as a set of false beliefs that would gradually fade as evolutionary ideas took hold. On the other side were humanistic atheists such as Marx, Nietzsche, and Freud, who understood god(s) as a projection of alienation and human suffering. In this mode of atheism, which was grounded in the human sciences, religion was understood as a social phenomenon. Instead of refuting theological claims as 'bad science,' these thinkers viewed religion as a response to social conditions and to anxieties that arose from them.

By centering divisions between scientific and humanistic atheism, LeDrew offers a useful template for thinking about the epistemological foundations that have informed the ideology of New Atheist thinkers. For example, he notes how their "understanding of evolution as a social process" lends itself to the view that "Islamic civilizations are 'backward' and 'uncivilized' and that the presence of Muslims in the West threatens our progress" (2015: 58). This type of social evolutionary thinking corresponds with older sociological theories of secularization that predicted the inevitable decline of religion (LeDrew 2016: 61–66). Unlike many sociologists of religion, however, the New Atheists do not grapple with the "centrality of practice, ritual, and community" (74), which most of the humanist theorists deem necessary for understanding what motivates religious groups. This also helps to explain why those who adhere to scientific atheism tend to favor liberal individualism in the politic realm, and reject multiculturalism and deliberative democracy (89), which are seen to promote cultural relativism and weaken the appeal of liberal and scientific principles.

One thing that hasn't been examined in this growing body of research is how atheist and other nonreligious identity formations have aligned and intersected with various online communities around a shared sense of Western identity and values. Although Cimino and Smith's *Atheist Awakening* (2014) provides an analysis of online atheist and secular humanist communities, the authors deliberately "take the focus off the culture wars" and look at the "'progressive' side" of these spaces in order to better understand processes of community building and collective identity formation (4).[8] By contrast, I am interested in exploring how Western civilizational rhetoric functions to unite certain atheist, secularist, and nonreligious identities (including ex-Muslims) as a form of cultural identity beyond the mere rejection of religion.

Classifying secular and nonreligious identities

In their recent study *None of the Above* (2020), Joel Thiessen and Sarah Wilkins-Laflamme classify nonreligious identity in the United States and Canada into five typologies, which they describe as: (1) Involved seculars (non-believers who are active in atheist, humanist, or secularist communities), which are relatively small; (2) Inactive non-believers (those who don't believe in God and don't do much about it); (3) Inactive believers (those who do believe in God and don't do much about it); (4) Spiritual but not religious (those who reject organized religion but express openness to various spiritual ideas); and (5) Involved believers (those who participate in a religious organization but do not identify with any one religion).

These kinds of distinctions have gained greater attention since 2012, when the Pew Forum on Religion & Public Life sparked interest in this topic after reporting that 1 in 5 Americans claim to have no religious identity (Pew Research Center 2012). This research has produced a number of novel typologies for thinking about the category 'nonreligion' (Baker & Smith 2015; Drescher 2016) and drawn attention to the fact that there is no necessary connection between a person's belief (or lack thereof) and their affiliation (or lack thereof). The initial research on the Nones, as Steven Ramey (2013) points out, revolved around people's response to one question: religious affiliation. For Ramey, classifying people based on this kind of broad criteria can lead to problematic assumptions about what binds a group together and, in some cases, may contribute to the creation of such identities, *ex nihilo*. At the same time, this data raises some interesting questions about the classification of secular identities. For example, do secular identities only include atheistic groups, be they of the scientific or humanist varieties, or do they encompass all those who express a dissatisfaction with organization religion?

Theissen and Wilkins-Laflamme's classification of "Involved seculars" calls attention to the relatively small percentage of atheists and humanists who actively engage with secular communities and organizations, especially when compared to the broader field of those who identify as nonreligious.[9] When considering those atheist and nonreligious identities that are not actively involved with an organized community, but might, for example, identify as atheist in their Twitter bios, it becomes even more difficult to generalize about shared beliefs and practices beyond the most basic criteria.

Although Theissen and Wilkins-Laflamme found a strong tendency toward liberal or progressive values among the Nones in their research (e.g., on issues such as abortion and LGBTQ+ rights), I would argue that such characterizations do not adequately account for the politics and ideologies of this broad group of people. For one thing, endorsing basic rights for women and for minority groups (like atheists) does not necessarily correspond with other progressive or left-leaning values. As nonreligious identities have become more socially accepted in the Euro-West, and as online spaces have reduced the need for many younger people to become actively involved with secular/humanist/atheist organizations, it stands to reason that we will continue to see a more heterogeneous mix of cultural and political values among the nonreligious. This recalls Tara Burton's (2020) characterization of "remixed cultures" (see chapter 1), particularly her emphasis on how online communities will often get their sense of community from one place and their sense of meaning from another.

Complicating matters further, the growth of atheist churches such as the Sunday Assembly (RT 2013), the development of 'secular spirituality,'[10] and groups like The Satanic Temple (TST), who perform rituals and adhere to seven core tenants, are further challenging the ways in which religion and nonreligion are categorized under law and in popular culture (Wikipedia 2021c).[11] The TST, for example, has argued for status as a religion in US courts to gain certain rights that are typically afforded to those who can claim a "sincerely held religious belief" (Laycock 2020). If these trends continue to multiply, so too will definitions of what constitutes a secular identity above and beyond the most basic criteria of something that we contrast with 'religion.'

Online atheism

Commenting on the effects of social media during the surge of street protests in the United States during the summer of 2020, journalist Zaid Jilani makes the following observation:

> Social media created a new environment where no matter what you believe you can go somewhere on the Internet and you can link up

> with other people . . . and bounce ideas off of them that they basically agree with. . . . And what makes matters worse is that some websites, like YouTube, actually have an algorithm that encourages polarization, because when you watch one video it'll send you another video that has a similar kind of political orientation. . . . It doesn't really suggest for you to watch something from the other point of view . . . The algorithm was designed to keeping pushing you further and further down the rabbit-hole.
>
> (Rising 2020)

In this interview, Jilani is concerned with how social media creates communication bubbles or silos, where people are increasingly fed information that confirms pre-existing biases and shores up tribalistic identities (typically described along a left/right axis). While there is a growing body of research on this phenomenon (Jenkins et al. 2013; Zuboff 2019), there is a lot that remains unclear about the relationship between online participation and identity formation. One thing that is becoming clearer, however, is that the algorithms Jilani writes about are designed to maximize screen time and feed ad revenues, which incentives outrage-producing 'click-bait' and in-group solidarity as viewers are encouraged to consume, 'like,' and comment on content that features a shared enemy. In this environment, recalling Taibbi's (2019) three 'massive revolutions' in media since the late 1980s (see chapter 1), nuanced debate has less currency as content creators are encouraged to promote 'intramural conflict' as the best way to be seen and heard.

The peak of New Atheism during the mid-to-late 2000s coincided with the height of the 'war on terror,' where leading figures were able to piggyback their message on top of widespread anti-Muslim sentiment in the Euro-West. It was also during this time that YouTube videos came into prominence, where figures like Dawkins, Hitchens, Harris, and Bill Maher became regular fixtures, appearing in streamed debates with theologians, on news shows, and in documentaries (often free online) to spread their message.[12] By the early 2010s, global uprisings like the Arab Spring and the Occupy movement displaced the centrality that Muslims/Islam had held in popular Euro-Western discourse since the 9/11 attacks, while a surge of new online forums elevated the perspectives of previously marginalized groups, including racialized, queer, feminist, and Muslim voices, along with 'trolls' (Phillips 2015), and even far-right militia groups (Neiwert 2017). In this context, debates over the existence of God or 'evolution versus creationism' seemed to have run out of steam,[13] giving way to a more diffuse set of identity-focused culture wars issues.[14]

Commenting on some of the ways that New Atheism has aligned with right-leaning identity politics on platforms like YouTube, Angela Nagle observes:

> It [the new atheism] was one of the predecessors to the alt-light, with an underlying Christopher Hitchens style of hitting out at the irrational and the faithful. All the 'Milo OWNS stupid feminist' type of videos today are made with much the same style as the new atheist videos that were equally numerous on YouTube a few years before with titles like "HITCHSLAP." Hitchens OWNS stupid Christian woman.
>
> (2017: 109)

The ubiquity of this type of identity-focused commentary on social media forums (e.g., left versus right) has grown exponentially in recent years, where the incentive to 'OWN' one's opponent will often take precedence over the ideals of skepticism and rational debate. Given the prevalence of right-leaning cultural politics among many prominent New Atheists (e.g., regarding feminism, gender identity, immigration, and Islam), it is not surprising that these commentators would find themselves more algorithmically aligned with figures and forums opposed to 'political correctness' and the alleged suppression of free speech by those who favor more culturally left-leaning ideas. Two contrasting examples that highlight these trends can be seen in the work of secular humanist Chris Stedman and with the controversy known as #elavatorgate.

In his book *Faitheist: How an Atheist Found Common Ground with the Religious* (2012), Stedman attempted to shift popular atheist rhetoric away from the confrontational style of debunking religious beliefs toward a focus on shared values between humanists and the religious. Despite some decent publicity for his book, including an interview with Bill O'Reilly on Fox News, Stedman's attempt at forging a new type of atheist identity did not seem to catch much steam, not least, perhaps, because he lacked an online presence and a 'clickable' message that fit with the logic and incentive structures of new media.

By contrast, Rebecca Watson, founder of the Skepchick blog and former cohost of *The Skeptics' Guide to the Universe* podcast, gained widespread attention back in 2011 when she video-blogged about feeling uncomfortable at a Center for Inquiry Conference in Dublin, Ireland, after a fellow conference-goer propositioned her alone in an elevator at 4:00 am. A deluge of hate mail followed in what became known as #elevatorgate, which spiked considerably after Richard Dawkins criticized Watson for "mocking Western feminists for complaining about such trivial things as be propositioned in an elevator, when much greater suffering was taking place in the Muslim world" (qtd. in Nagle, 109–10).[15] More recently at the secular conference Mythicist Milwaukee in 2017, atheist podcaster Thomas Smith challenged prominent skeptic Sargon of Akkad to account for his Tweet to British politician Jess Phillips stating, "I wouldn't even rape you," which was accompanied by the hashtag #FeminismIsCancer. Much of the crowd cheered in support of Sargon's statement, to which Smith berated them in dis-belief, lamenting, "is this what the atheist scene has become?" (Polite Conversations 2017d). Although the type of secular humanism that Stedman promoted in the early 2010s has developed new strains in recent years, the prevalence of culturally right-leaning identity politics has continued to dominate in online atheist spaces up to the present.

Atheism and the alt-right/lite

In recent years, the neologisms 'alt-right' and 'alt-lite' (Stern 2019; Hawley 2019) have marked the political landscape in a variety of ways and bare some overlapping affinities with movement atheism and the so-called Intellectual Dark Web (IDW). The term 'IDW' was coined by mathematician Eric Weinstein, popularized by former *New York Times* communist Bari Weiss (2018), and has been used to identify a group of academics and political commentators who are united around shared concerns over the presumed excesses of left-leaning identity politics, especially on college campuses. For some IDW figures, the influence of postmodernism and 'cultural Marxism' is said to be particularly dangerous, contributing to moral relativism, political correctness, and the stifling of free speech. Here the overlap with early New Atheist rhetoric is discernable, as are several key figures. According to Weiss, the so-called New Atheists Ayaan Hirsi Ali, Sam Harris, Steven Pinker, and Maajid Nawaz are counted among its ranks, along with Douglas Murray, Jordan Peterson, and prominent American commentators Joe Rogan, Ben Shapiro, and Dave Rubin, among others. While most of these figures identify as atheist, two of the more popular (and more conservative) among them, Jordan Peterson and Ben Shapiro identify as Christian and Jewish, respectively.

When considering the shift among popular atheist figures like Harris and Hirsi Ali toward working with the so-called religious moderates who share secular Western values (to be discussed in the next section), these alliances are not surprising. What is more surprising are the findings of a comprehensive 2019 study which argues that the IDW "is a gateway to the far right" (Dickson 2019). While IDW figures do not espouse white supremacy or ethno-nationalism explicitly, tend to uphold some version of civic nationalism, and vocally distance themselves from the 'alt-right,' there is a discernable overlap in some of their talking points. This can be seen with debates concerning gender and trans-identities, feminism and race science, masculinity and men's rights, along with a disdain for leftists and, in some cases, migrants and Muslims.[16] As Alexandra Stern (2019) argues, alt-lite (and IDW) figures tend to embrace gay men and men of color into their ranks (e.g., Murray and Rubin identify as gay), while at the same time dismissing concerns about gender, trans, and racial inequalities that push beyond basic rights as an excessive by-product of college leftists and 'social justice warriors.'

These identity-fueled culture wars continue to have widespread appeal, especially since the election of Donald Trump (Brooks 2020).[17] Indeed, for many who have engaged with atheist ideas online since the late 2000s, the prevalence of blasphemy in popular Anglo-American spaces has lost much of its edginess, where antipathy toward religion represents only one facet of atheist identities – and in many cases, one that is not all that important. Asking whether this is also true for ex-Muslims is a question that I now turn to.

Some ex-Muslim assemblages

Sam Harris and the embrace of 'moderate' Muslims

After nearly a decade of promoting the idea that religion must be overcome if science and reason are to flourish (Harris 2006),[18] Sam Harris changed tack by collaborating with self-described secular Muslim Maajid Nawaz in their book *Islam and the Future of Tolerance: A Dialogue* (Harris & Nawaz 2014). This was the first example of a New Atheist figure joining forces with a practicing Muslim in print in an attempt to promote the idea of cooperation on the basis of shared values. In the course of their exchange, Nawaz describes his aims as follows:

> What I hope is that people will arrive not just at secularism, but also at democratic and human rights values. So the task ahead of us is monumental, but secularism is the prerequisite. This is a unique challenge for Muslims today owing to the rise of Islamism and jihadism, and to the historically European context in which secularism is framed. This challenge is not, however, insurmountable.
>
> (30)

Although this collaboration with a 'moderate Muslim' marks a sea-change from the chaos rhetoric of "the end of faith" (Harris 2004), Harris's shift was not an embrace of humanistic atheism by any stretch. Instead, it was a recognition on Harris's part that religion was not going to disappear and must, therefore, be dealt with in some other way. This meant that 'good'

Muslims no longer need to renounce Islam to be considered proper secular subjects, but instead must embrace secular values, such as democracy and human rights, and be willing to call-out 'bad' Muslims of various stripes.

Prior to his collaboration with Nawaz, Harris could only point to ex-Muslim Ayaan Hirsi Ali among his ranks, who is not exactly a poster child for tolerance. By appealing to 'moderate Muslims' who share secular values, New Atheists like Harris were better able to counter accusations of Islamophobia, and position themselves as defenders of individual freedom for *all* Muslims over and against the so-called regressive left (Wikipedia 2021).[19] Seeing as 'secular values' like individual freedom are also a central plank in many ex-Muslim narratives, this discourse has a certain appeal, especially if we consider ex-Muslim as a transitional identity for those who have recently rejected Islam, and who are eager to ally with those voices who appear to validate their anger and negative experiences.

Ayaan Hirsi Ali: from Nomad to Heretic

Raised Muslim in Somalia, Saudi Arabia, Ethiopia, and Kenya, Hirsi Ali applied for political asylum in the Netherlands at the age of twenty-three, where she received a university education in philosophy and eventually served in the Dutch Parliament. She would later immigrate to the United States after the murder of Theo van Gogh, with whom she codirected a short documentary critical of Islam called *Submission* (Buruma 2007). Hirsi Ali recounts her experiences as a youth in *The Caged Virgin* (2008), including undergoing genital mutilation/cutting; her transition away from Islam in *Infidel* (2008); her migration to the United States in *Nomad* (2011); and presents her most prescriptive argument in *Heretic: Why Islam Needs a Reformation Now* (2015).

Like Harris, Hirsi Ali has undergone a change in perspective in recent years, from calling for the abolition of religion, and suggesting that moderate Muslims convert to Christianity (following the premise that it is more compatible with secular values), to her current view that seeks to differentiate three types of Muslims – Medina, Mecca, and Modifying Muslims. Medina Muslims are violent and extremist, while Mecca Muslims shy away from violence and can thus be reformed. Modifying Muslims, including moderates and Ex-Muslims, are considered the ideal and are who her book is primarily aimed at reforming.

Hirsi Ali is a fascinating case study on the intersections between movement atheism, Ex-Muslims, and the political spectrum from alt-lite to alt-right. Along with Canadian journalist Irshad Manji (2003), who identifies as a queer woman and describes herself as a "Muslim refusenik," Hirsi Ali was among the first authors in North America with a Muslim background to produce a best-selling book on her traumatic experiences under 'Islam.' She was quickly adopted by the New Atheists and was courted by a variety of commentators and lobbying groups, such as the conservative American Enterprise Institute, with whom she has come to identify over and against the 'regressive left.' Like many New Atheist figures, Hirsi Ali is not merely known for her strong rejection of Islam, but increasingly for her brand of Western-centric identity politics that promotes 'secular values' in the form of free market capitalism, individualism, and military intervention as a remedy to Islamic extremism.

Ali Rizvi: the atheist Muslim

Like Hirsi Ali, Ali Rizvi was raised Muslim in a Muslim-majority country (Saudi Arabia) before immigrating to Canada. Rizvi is a trained medical doctor and, while not as well known as Hirsi Ali, gained considerable attention for his book *The Atheist Muslim: A Journey from Religion to Reason* (2016). Indeed, the endorsements on the back cover reflect a who's-who of New Atheist and IDW personalities, including Dawkins, Harris, Nawaz, Steven Pinker, Jerry Coyne, and Dave Rubin. In this sense, Rizvi's reception is very much linked to the politics of New Atheism.

In his opening chapter, Rizvi positions himself between the 'left,' who are deemed too soft on Islam, and conservatives of all stripes, who trade in bigotry and, most importantly, fail to adhere to secular principles grounded in science and reason. While Rizvi concedes that Western colonialism and imperialism have contributed to violence "in the name of religion," he maintains that the "root cause" of these problems lies with Islam itself. Part of his reason for this view comes from experiences with Muslim family and friends blaming "rise of militant Islamic fervor in the world" on everything "but the religion itself" (28). Rizvi is thus motivated by a desire to challenge moderate and even progressive Muslims who "soften and egalitarianize the harshness of [their] ancient book" (172). For these and other reasons, he proposes a four-step process for the Muslim world: a rejection of scriptural inerrancy; reformation; secularism; and Enlightenment (202).

While some of these arguments can be found in the pages of Harris or Hirsi Ali, one thing that is novel in Rizvi's approach is his insistence on distinguishing between Islam as a set of *ideas* and an *ideology*, and Muslims as a *people* and a *community* (96). As an ex-Muslim of Pakistani heritage, Rizvi is sensitive to anti-Muslim bigotry and has maintained close ties with many Muslims. Unlike some ex-Muslims, then, Rizvi's identity is not characterized by a rejection of Muslims as a people and a community, but rather one of an accomplished doctor and writer who aims to build upon New

Atheist ideas in the interest of promoting alternatives for Muslims and, ultimately, a secular reformation for Islam.

Like the New Atheists, Rizvi rejects the term Islamophobia, which he views as the province of the "regressive left" who conflate "anti-Muslim bigotry" with the critique of "ideas" (148). Despite his efforts to distinguish between critiquing Islam and bigotry toward Muslims, Rizvi's indebtedness to scientific atheism and rhetorical appeals to Western values resembles the kind of "patriotic atheism" that Bullivant (2010) points to as a defining characteristic of New Atheist ideology. This can be seen, for example, when he writes:

> Many liberals also seemed to excuse any atrocity committed in the name of Islam as some kind of reaction to Western imperialism or U.S. foreign policy. Of course, they weren't completely wrong. . . . Islamic fundamentalist governments and militant groups alike use this far-left narrative of victimization to deflect criticism and further justify oppressing their own people.
>
> (136–7)

Putting aside these partisan comments against the so-called far-left, Rizvi's firsthand experience with this anti-imperialist rhetoric in Saudi Arabia offers a window into what motivates some of the ressentiment that many ex-Muslims feel toward certain liberal-left commentators who are willing to critique Islamophobia but not Islamic ideas.

Despite Rizvi's generalizations about the so-called regressive left, his concerns point to a basic problem in Euro-Western debates on Islam – namely, a widespread ignorance of Islamic theologies and Muslim cultures. This problem, I suggest, contributes to the perpetuation of simplified representations of good versus bad Muslims, and incentivizes one-side commentary against one's imagined political adversaries over critical engagement and analysis. For this reason, it is worth paying attention to the very real and felt ressentiment that many ex-Muslims like Rizvi feel about their own experiences under authoritarian Islamic governments and communities. These experiences are fuel for apostasy and help to explain why many ex-Muslims prefer scientific atheism over humanistic approaches, and often align with those on the cultural right, despite the racial overtones of their anti-Muslim rhetoric.

Apostates and other ex's

The first collection of ex-Muslim testimonies in the English language comes from Ibn Warraq's edited volume *Leaving Islam: Apostates Speak Out* (2003), where he provides testimonials from his organization *The Institute for the Secularisation of Islamic Society* (ISIS) (chapter 2); from born Muslims (chapter 3); and from Western converts to Islam who have since left. In his introduction to chapter 3, Ibn Warraq likens Islam to communism, and cautions that unless Islam is reformed soon a battle will ensue "between Islam and Western democracy" (Loc. 1545). In the final section of his book, "Ex-Muslims of the World Unite," Ibn Warraq lists a large number of organizations that prospective apostates can go to "for spiritual and intellectual sustenance once one has abandoned Islam" (Loc. 41).

With the exception of Ibn Warraq's own organization (ISIS), which stresses the need to transform Islamic societies to respect the rights of the individual, and promote "the ideas of rationalism, secularism, democracy and human rights" (5909), other organizations that he endorses, such as *Faith Freedom International* and *Apostates of Islam*, focus on the "evils" of Islam in civilizational terms (e.g., as a war between "the civilized world and barbarity"). This tension between encouraging reform in Muslim-majority countries and playing on fears of a 'clash of civilizations' is characteristic of many higher profile ex-Muslim narratives. While most ex-Muslims do embrace 'secularism' as a path toward individual freedoms, many reject the confrontational rhetoric that is found among the most vocal figures.

The only book-length academic treatment of ex-Muslims to date is *The Apostates: When Muslims Leave Islam* (2015) by Simon Cottee, which he describes "as a corrective to the neglect of Islamic apostasy in sociology" (2), where the focus has been on conversion to – but not apostasy from – Islam. Distinguishing his work from polemical figures such as Ibn Warraq and Ayaan Hirsi Ali, Cottee approaches his topic through a qualitative sociology, interviewing 35 ex-Muslims in the UK and Canada on the "lived realities of apostates and how they subjectively make sense of their situation" (4).

Cottee expressed difficulty in finding a large enough sample of ex-Muslims to interview for his book and was only able to find respondents by mining the online forums of the *Council of Ex-Muslims of Britain* or CEMB (founded in 2007 by Maryam Namazie), which he describes as "a self-help refuge for secular and non-religious ex-Muslims," and *Faith Freedom International* (started by Ali Sina in 2001) based in the United States, which "is more squarely a site for political engagement and discussion" (6). By centering the narratives of participants on these online forums, Cottee aims to fill a gap in scholarship by exploring "the social situation of ordinary non-activist ex-Muslims," as opposed to "career apostates" who tend to get the most attention in the media (8).[20]

Narratives of "career apostates" like Hirsi Ali and Rizvi tend to promote hostility toward their former religion, which helps them gain attention from non-Muslims in a media ecosystem that rewards controversy and outrage. The stated motivations that Cottee found among his interviewees, however, were more mixed. Although most of them were aware of "career apostates" and credit "coming into contact with irreligious source-material" as helping their transition from one group identity to another (156), it was not clear that most of them identify as ex-Muslim beyond participation in these online forums.

Cottee draws on Stuart A. Wright's distinction between 'typical' and 'leavetaker' apostates to mark an important difference among his interviewees, where leavetakers are defined as those who make a public act of their opposition to their former affiliation and thus embrace "a posture of confrontation" (qtd. in Cottee, 16). While agreeing that apostasy is more in-line with this latter stance, Cottee stresses that apostates might also join another group ('religious' or 'secular'), remain unaffiliated, independent, leave for principled or pragmatic reasons (e.g., to exit a bad situation or improve their material interests elsewhere) and, in some cases (common among ex-Muslims) retain nominal affiliation (i.e., as Muslim) for fear of retribution (e.g., from one's family, community, and government authorities) (17). Cottee also observed a desire among many of his interviewees to "move on" from the ex-Muslim label as they felt it was holding them back from creating a newer, more stable identity (206).

These sentiments speak to the transitional nature of the term ex-Muslim, which parallels other 'ex' identities such as ex-evangelicals and ex-Mormons. As Seth Payne (2013) remarks in his study on ex-Mormons, they "are often motivated to disseminate and produce exit narratives" that trace their trajectory from "victims to victors" (85). The 'ex' or 'apostate' label is often temporary, however, and is "rarely . . . a key identity marker" as individuals who use this term tend to develop a new religious or nonreligious identity (Cragun 2014: vi).[21] In this sense, it is worth asking what factors drive the performance of ex-Muslim identities beyond the more familiar motivations of "career apostates," and the initial appeal of aligning with a supportive community that can aid the transition away from Islam?

Maria Vliek's studies on ex-Muslims (2019) and ex-Muslim organizations (2018) in Britain and the Netherlands offer some useful insights here by showing how the particular models of state secularism in Britain and the Netherlands shape the narratives and priorities of these groups. Whereas British ex-Muslim organizations like the CEMB have been critical of multiculturalism in the UK as too accommodating of conservative Muslims, and are thus more militant in their approach, groups in the Netherlands were primarily concerned with how their public statements could be used in the service of anti-Muslim bigotry (e.g., from Geert Wilders Party for Freedom). If domestic politics is a useful metric for tracking the kind of public narratives and interests that inform ex-Muslim organizations, this does not tell us much about those who may use the ex-Muslim label individually but are not active in political campaigns. In this sense, the confrontational or 'leavetaker' approach of many ex-Muslim organizations parallels the incentive structures of online identification, be it an individual's Twitter persona or pages on social media forums such as Facebook and Instagram.

Polite conversations

Eiynah began *Polite Conversation* in February of 2016 and continues to produce shows on a regular basis.[22] She was raised in a liberal Muslim Pakistani family in a compound near Jeddah, Saudi Arabia, spent some of her high school years in Pakistan, and migrated to Toronto in her late teens. Shortly after moving to Canada, she renounced Islam and began to identify as an ex-Muslim atheist. Eiynah's stated goal in starting *Polite Conversations* was to help normalize the idea of apostasy and create space for more liberal Muslim voices to be heard.

Beginning with her first episode on February 22, 2016 ("Maryam Namazie"), Eiynah's topical focus revolved around a particular set of themes, including the importance of free speech and blasphemy, deradicalization, promoting ex-Muslims and others who have left Judaism and Zoroastrianism, two interviews with the co-founder of The Satanic Temple Lucien Greaves, several features on women in Saudi Arabia, 'reformist Muslims' like Irshad Manji, deconversion narratives with fellow ex-Muslims Ali Rizvi, Sarah Haider, and Maryam Namazie, and more. She also had two heated conversations with the right-leaning Muslim critic of Islam Tarek Fatah and self-proclaimed Islamophobe Robert Spencer. Topics on veiling controversies (hijab, niqab, burkini) were also prominent, as were questions surrounding queerness, trans-issues, feminism, leftist in-fighting, and how to be allied with liberal Muslims and ex-Muslims without propping up conservative ideas. One example of this last theme can be found in her interview with sex-advice columnist Dan Savage from January 2017, where Eiynah introduces the show as "an honest conversation about the left's response to minorities within minorities like ex-Muslims, even Muslims who are critical of things like homophobia, misogyny within their religion." Behind this particular narrative is a frustration with the 'left' and its unwillingness (or inability) to critique Islam. This fact, she claims, is part of the reason why New Atheists such as Dawkins, Harris, and Hitchens are so appealing to ex-Muslims and echoes some of the concerns of Hirsi Ali and Rizvi noted in the previous sections.

Following the election of Donald Trump, a noticeable shift in Eiynah's commentary began to emerge, as seen in an episode on October 12, 2017, where she states:

> Now, as the political climate changes in the West, we see some cracks in the ex/reformist Muslim movement more obviously than ever. There were those of us who were coming at it from the angle of opposing conservatism, whatever form it may take, generally pushing for more progressive values. And others who were specifically only opposing Islam. And as a result, the people who prioritize opposing Islam alone are happy now to ally with the Western right.
>
> (Polite Conversations 2017d)

Here we see one of the first public statements by Eiynah marking a distinction between those whose leavetaking of Islam was grounded in a more "progressive" understanding of secular values and those whose transformation has been characterized by a willingness to ally with those who espouse anti-Muslim sentiment.

Another example of this shift in focus is from a panel discussion titled "Free Speech: the right versus SJWs," (Polite Conversations 2017b) where Eiynah and her guests discuss the lop-sided attention paid to the so-called free speech controversies on the 'left' by numerous movement atheist figures, including a "disproportionate focus on every campus kid that does something ridiculous," while at the same time downplaying racism, Trumpism, and sexism. As she states in another episode from March of 2020, titled "The Online World of Muslims":

> Before it just used to be shitting on creationists and making fun of Muslims and things like that. But that has come with a whole additional set of politics now, which means that you're likely going to be anti-trans, anti-feminist, anti-left.
>
> (Polite Conversations 2020)

This type of "anti-left" politics is attributed by Eiynah to a number of factors, not least of which is the way that online communities and algorithms have linked popular atheist rhetoric to alt-right and IDW figures who are regularly appealed to as respected Western intellectuals. The appeal of these intellectuals is also seen among ex-Muslims in Pakistan and Saudi Arabia, which Eiynah suggests is indicative of the reach of conservative politics online. As she puts it, "Just because they're getting solidarity in the Islam-bashing they get caught up in their other politics too, not realizing how they've just come full circle; how they abandoned all the principles they claimed to have left Islam because of" (Polite Conversations 2019b).

Eiynah's emphasis on secular principles was a central component of her initial motivation for identifying as an atheist and ex-Muslim and helps to explain her ambivalence toward these labels in recent years given the apparent shift toward right-leaning culture wars politics, especially in online spaces. One episode that highlights this angle is a conversation with podcaster Thomas Smith discussing his debate with skeptic Sargon of Aakad at the 2017 Mythicist Miliwaukee (MM) conference, where, as previously noted, Sargon was challenged by Smith on his comment to British MP Jess Philips, "I wouldn't even rape you." The supportive reaction by much of the audience, along with the endorsement of Sargon by MM in the first place, was seen as confirmation that the strong anti-feminist and anti-left currents online had migrated into active community spaces. As Eiynah puts it, "There's a deep, dogmatic resistance to criticism or self-reflection" in the so-called skeptic community (Polite Conversations 2017c). In this context, the stated values on the MM website in support of humanism, reason, logic, research, ethnic equality, and LGBTQ+ equality are seen to be shibboleths of an imagined value set that no longer holds in practice (Mythinformed 2021).

Eiynah maintains her earlier discomfort with Western media representations of Islam as 'peaceful' and (often) glorifying the hijab and niqab, in an ongoing effort to normalize what we might call 'queer' or dissenting Muslims and ex-Muslims against the prevailing liberal orthodoxies of good versus bad Muslims. As she states in her April 2019 episode, "The Christchurch attack and online radicalization":

> I'm fighting for more diverse representation of Muslims in the media . . . to show only conservative Muslims, as often the CBC does . . . and they don't show trans Muslims, gay Muslims, progressive Muslims, it's always this caricature, this one-dimensional [portrayal] that conservative equals Muslim.
>
> (Polite Conversations 2019a)

Eiynah continues to negotiate her desire for a more diverse representation of Muslims with episodes such as "Masturbating while Muslim," "Sex, Booze, Ramadan, and Eating Disorders," and "Asifa Lahore – British Muslim Transgender Drag Queen." At the same time, she reluctantly maintains the label ex-Muslim, as stated in a 2020 Patron Skype Chat:

> But if there's no one without this false centrist or rightwing politics; no one calling themselves ex-Muslim then the people who are wanting to leave Islam will only see these grifting types around them, and they won't have anyone to identify with, even if they don't want to call themselves

> ex-Muslim . . . because that's the problem. There's so many good ex-Muslims out there with decent . . . values, but they don't' vocalize their ex-Muslim status because people on the right fetishize ex-Muslims.

By maintaining the label ex-Muslim, Eiynah sees herself as providing an alternative to right-leaning forces in the atheist and ex-Muslim scene. Despite numerous conversations with disenchanted atheists, she has not found other self-identifying ex-Muslims that share her views, or at least not one's who are willing or able to do so on her show.

Since the fall of 2020, Eiynah has begun a series called 'Woking Up' on Sam Harris, who she first interviewed back in 2016 (Harris). While admitting to being a former Harris fan, this series, which boasts four episodes at the time of this writing, stands as a testimonial of her own transition away from New Atheist ideology. Increasingly, Eiynah's guests and patrons reflect not only left-leaning cultural politics but also left and democratic socialist ideas, which points to newer realignments among many on the 'left' online scene following the influence of Bernie Sanders beginning in 2016. Although she continues to focus on cultural issues on her podcast, these trends parallel the kind of realignments that many left-leaning atheist commentators have followed, where, as Eiynah herself puts it,

> Initially, it was very cathartic to me to be angry and lash out at religion because of growing up in a theocracy. But then, a year or two into it, you're like, no big deal. Creationism is ridiculous, yes, we know religion isn't real, God isn't real, ok, now what? Can we talk about something else now?
>
> (Polite Conversations 2021)

Conclusion

In this chapter, I have attempted to sketch out some discursive and ideological shifts in movement atheist and ex-Muslim identities in the post-9/11 and Trump eras. Here I've noted how the earlier rhetoric of 'Western values' as an embodiment of secular reason has shifted toward narratives that prioritize identity politics, revealing the shaky foundation of movement atheism as a lodestar of principled secular reason. Among other things, these ideological and rhetorical realignments highlight the role of political subjectivity in shaping the boundaries of 'religion,' religious, and nonreligious identities and reveal, in the case of Eiynah, how categories like atheist and ex-Muslim are conditioned just as much by the vagaries of culture as they are by some imagined, stable set of beliefs and principles that are commonly said to define them.

Notes

1 Movement atheism is a loosely defined term describing the interactions between atheist thought leaders, organizations, conferences, in magazines, and online (blogs, social media sites, etc.).
2 LeDrew (2015) defines scientism as "a belief in the epistemic authority of the natural sciences over and above all other forms of understanding, which in practice also amounts to the political authority of the natural sciences" (57).
3 See Laurence Moore and Isaac Kramnick (2018) for an overview of atheist organizations in the US.
4 See Connolly's *Capitalism and Christianity* (2008).
5 Identity politics is a fraught term (see Haider 2018). I use it here to refer to public discourses that focus on conflicts surrounding racial, gender, and sexual identity, often to the exclusion of debates over public policy and other forms of building social solidarity.
6 For analysis on how self-described atheists and humanist organizations responded to the New Atheists, see Cimino and Smith (2014), esp. chapters 2 and 3; Moore and Kramnick, esp. chapter 8 (2018).
7 This view is also consistent with Cimino and Smith's findings, where they note how atheist political affiliations range "from the standard categories of socialist, progressive, libertarian, and conservative, to more idiosyncratic" (2014: 105).
8 In her forthcoming book *Practicing Atheism* (2021) Hannah Schneidt examines organized online atheist communities, with an emphasis on tensions between atheist cultures and mainstream religions.
9 This corresponds with Lois Lee's (2015) distinction between "substantial" and "insubstantial" secularism.
10 See chapter 4 of Cimino and Smith (2014), where they discuss ritualization among secular communities, such as pushing for the observance of Winter Solstice Day and celebrating Darwin Day (61).
11 The Wikipedia page for The Satanic Temple describe them as a "nontheistic religious group" (Wikipedia 2021c).
12 See Richard Dawkins documentary *The Root of all Evil* (2006) and Bill Maher's *Religulous* (2008).
13 See, for example, the 2008 documentary *Expelled: No Intelligence Allowed.* Reviewing this film for their podcast Michael and Us (2018), Luke Savage and Will Sloan argue that *Expelled* was a last gasp in the 'evolution versus creationism' debate from the cultural right and a harbinger of the free speech-focused culture wars that were to follow.
14 Sam Harris' popular podcast Making Sense (formerly called Waking Up) is perhaps the best-known example of this trend. One example of this shift from critiquing religion to a focus on politics and culture from the left of the spectrum is the popular YouTube program Secular Talk, which was founded in 2008. Also reflective of this shift are left-leaning YouTube programs such as The Young Turks and The David Pakman Show.
15 See Cimino and Smith (2014: 96) for a discussion of other controversies involving misogyny and harassment in movement atheism.
16 For example, Harris, Murray, and Shapiro have all expressed anti-immigrant and anti-Muslim sentiment.
17 For a critique of the IDW, see Michael Brooks' *Against the Web* (2020).

18 See Harris's *Letter to a Christian Nation* (2006) for a book-length example of this conflict-driven narrative.
19 This term was coined by Nawaz to describe "a section of left-wing politics, who are accused of holding views, such as tolerating Islamism or opposition to free speech, that conflict with liberal principles" (Wikipedia 2020).
20 British journalist Hussain Kesvani (2019) found similar tendencies among ex-Muslims in London, who "felt more comfortable in private chat rooms, Facebook and WhatsApp groups, and on the tightly moderated ex-Muslim subreddit, than on other, more public, social media" (217).
21 There is no Wikipedia page for Ex-Muslims, but there is a site labeled "List of Former Muslims" (Wikipedia 2021a). Among the categories listed on this page are: "Converted to an Abrahamic Religion"; Converted to an Indian Religion"; and "Part of an unorganized Religion or no religion." The latter includes sub-categories for atheists, agnostics, deists, nonreligious; and 'Other,' which emphasize 'new age' type affiliations.
22 At the time of this writing there are 62 PC episodes, 23 panels (featuring 2–3 guests), and a handful of AMAs (ask me anything), Patron Skype chats, commentaries, and speeches. In addition, Eiynah has an ongoing series called Woking Up, which provides a critique of Sam Harris.

Works cited

Amarasingam, A., ed. 2010. *Religion and the New Atheism: A Critical Appraisal*. Leiden: Brill.

Baker, J., Smith, B. 2015. *American Secularism: Cultural Contours of Nonreligious Belief Systems*. New York: New York University Press.

Bayart, J. F. 2005. *The Illusion of Cultural Identity*. Chicago: University of Chicago Press.

Beredjick, C. 2017. *Queer Disbelief: Why LGBTQ Equality Is an Atheist Issue*. Chicago: Friendly Atheist Press.

Brooks, M. 2020. *Against the Web: A Cosmopolitan Answer to the New Right*. Hampshire, UK: Zero Books.

Bullivant, S. 2010. The New Atheism and Sociology: Why Here? Why Now? What Next? In: A. Amarasingam, ed., *Religion and the New Atheism: A Critical Appraisal*. Leiden: Brill, pp. 109–124.

Bullivant, S. 2020. Explaining the Rise of "Nonreligion Studies": Subfield Formation and Institutionalization within the Sociology of Religion. *Social Compass*, 67(1), pp. 86–102.

Bullivant, S., Tomlins, S. 2016. *The Atheist Bus Campaign: Global Manifestations and Responses*. Leiden: Brill.

Burton, T. 2020. *Strange Rites: New Religions for a Godless World*. New York: Hachette Book Group.

Buruma, I. 2007. *Murder in Amsterdam: Liberal Europe, Islam, and the Limits of Tolerance*. New York: Penguin Books.

Cameron, C. 2019. *Black Freethinkers: A History of African American Secularism*. Evanston: Northwestern University Press.

Cavanaugh, W. 2009. *The Myth of Religious Violence: Secular Ideology and the Roots of Modern Conflict*. New York: Oxford University Press.

Cimino, R., Smith, C. 2011. The New Atheism and the Formation and the Imagined Secularist Community. *Journal of Media and Religion*, 10(1), pp. 24–38.

Cimino, R., Smith, C. 2014. *Atheist Awakening: Secular Activism and Community in America*. New York: Oxford University Press.

Connolly, W. 2008. *Capitalism and Christianity: American Style*. Durham: Duke University Press.

Cottee, S. 2015. *The Apostates: When Muslims Leave Islam*. London: Hurst & Company.

Cragun, R. 2014. "Apostates", "Anti-Mormons", and Other Problems in Seth Payne's "Ex-Mormon Narratives and Pastoral Apologetics". *Dialogue: A Journal of Mormon Thought*, 47(2), pp. v–xxii.

Dawkins, R. 2006. *The God Delusion*. New York: Haughton Mifflin Company.

Dawkins, R. 2006. The Root of All Evil? Channel 4, UK. [Documentary].

Dennett, D. 2006. *Breaking the Spell: Religion as a Natural Phenomenon*. New York: Viking Press.

Dickson, E. J. 2019. Study Shows How the Intellectual Dark Web Is a Gateway to the Far-Right. *Rolling Stone*, August 28. Available at: www.rollingstone.com/culture/culture-news/youtube-far-right-radicalization-study-877061/ [Accessed 20 January 2021].

Dickson, R. 2010. Religion as Phantasmagoria: Islam in the End of Faith. In: A. Amarasingam, ed., *Religion and the New Atheism: A Critical Appraisal*. Leiden: Brill, pp. 37–56.

Drescher, E., 2016. *Choosing Our Religion: The Spiritual Lives of Americans*. New York: Oxford University Press.

Eagleton, T. 2010. *Reason, Faith, and Revolution: Reflections on the God Debate*. New Haven: Yale University Press.

Fry, S. 2019. Forward. In: C. Hitchens, R. Dawkins, S. Harris, and D. Dennett, eds., *The Four Horsemen: The Conversations That Sparked an Atheist Revolution*. New York: Random House.

Gaylor, A. L. 1997. *Women without Superstition: No Gods: No Masters*. Ann Arbor: Freedom from Religion Foundation.

Haider, A. 2018. *Mistaken Identity: Race and Class in the Age of Trump*. London: Verso.

Harris, S. 2004. *The End of Faith: Religion, Terror, and the Future of Terror*. New York: W.W. Norton & Company.

Harris, S. 2006. *Letter to a Christian Nation*. New York: Vintage Books.

Harris, S., Nawaz, M., 2015. *Islam and the Future of Tolerance: A Dialogue*. Cambridge: Harvard University Press.

Haught, J. F. 2008. *God and the New Atheism: A Critical Response to Dawkins, Harris, and Hitchens*. Louisville: Westminster John Knox Press.

Hawley, G. 2019. *The Alt-Right: What Everyone Needs to Know*. New York: Oxford University Press.

Hedges, C. 2009. *When Atheism Becomes Religion*. New York: Simon & Schuster.

Hirsi Ali, A. 2008. *The Caged Virgin: An Emancipation Proclamation for Women and Islam*. New York: Atria Books.

Hirsi Ali, A. 2015. *Heretic: Why Islam Needs a Reformation Now*. New York: Harper Collins.

Hirsi Ali, A. 2008. *Infidel.* New York: Atria Books.

Hirsi Ali, A. 2011. *Nomad: A Personal Journey Through the Clash of Civilizations*. New York: Simon & Schuster.

Hitchens, C. 2007. *God Is Not Great: How Religious Poisons Everything*. New York: Twelve Books.

Jenkins, H., Ford, S., Green, J. 2013. *Spreadable Media: Creating Value and Meaning in a Networked Culture*. New York: New York University Press.

Johnson, A., Shirazi, N. 2019. The New Atheists: Celebrity Crusaders for Empire. *Citations Needed* [podcast], October 11. Available at: https://citationsneeded.libsyn.com/episode-12-new-atheist-celebrities-crusaders-for-empire [Accessed 20 January 2021].

Kesvani, H. 2019. *Follow Me, Akhi: The Online World of British Muslims*. London: Hurst & Company.

Laycock, J. 2020. *Speak of the Devil: How the Satanic Temple Is Changing the Way We Talk about Religion.* New York: Oxford University Press.

LeDrew, S. 2015. Atheism versus Humanism: Ideological Tensions and Identity Dynamics. In: L. Beaman, S. Tomlins, eds., *Atheist Identities: Spaces and Social Contexts*. Switzerland: Springer International Publishing, pp. 53–68.

LeDrew, S. 2016. *The Evolution of Atheism: The Politics of a Modern Movement*. New York: Oxford University Press.

Lee, L. 2015. *Recognizing the Non-Religious: Reimagining the Secular*. New York: Oxford University Press.

Maher, B. 2008. Religulous. Lions Gate Entertainment. [Documentary].

Manji, I. 2003. *The Trouble with Islam*. Toronto: Vintage Canada.

McGrath, A. 2007. *The Dawkins Delusion? Atheist Fundamentalism and the Denial of the Divine*. London: Society for Promoting Christian Knowledge.

Moore, R., Kramnick, I. 2018. *Godless Citizens in a Godly Republic: Atheists in American Public Life*. New York: W.W. Norton & Company.

Mythinformed. 2021. Who We Are. Available at: https://mythinformed.org [Accessed 20 January 2021].

Nagle, A. 2017. *Kill All Normies: Online Culture Wars from 4Chan and Tumblr to Trump and the Alt-Right.* Portland: Zero Books.

Neiwert, D. 2017. *Alt-America: The Rise of the Radical Right in the Age of Donald Trump*. London: Verso.

Payne, S. 2013. Ex-Mormon Narratives and Pastoral Apologetics. *Dialogue: A Journal of Mormon Thought*, 46(4), pp. 85–121.

Pew Research Center. 2012. “Nones” on the Rise. *Pew Research Center: Religion & Public Life*, October 9. Available at: www.pewforum.org/2012/10/09/nones-on-the-rise/ [Accessed 20 January 2021].

Phillips, W. 2015. *This Is Why We Can't Have Nice Things: Mapping the Relationship between Online Trolling and Mainstream Culture*. Cambridge: MIT Press.

Polite Conversations. 2016a. Maryam Namazie. Available at: https://soundcloud.com/nicemangos/polite-conversations-episode-1-maryam-namazie [Accessed 20 January 2021].

Polite Conversations. 2016b. Sam Harris. Available at: www.youtube.com/watch?v=AZVh_asjiK8 [Accessed 20 January 2021].

Polite Conversations. 2017a. Antifa and the Far Right in Canada. Available at: https://soundcloud.com/politeconversations/episode-24-dan-savage [Accessed 20 January 2021].

Polite Conversations. 2017b. Free Speech: The Right vs. SJWs. Available at: https://soundcloud.com/politeconversations/pc-panel-discussion-6-free-speech-the-right-vs-sjws [Accessed 20 January 2021].

Polite Conversations. 2017c. Mythicist MilWhatHappened? Available at: https://soundcloud.com/politeconversations/episode-39-mythicist-milwhathappened [Accessed 20 January 2021].

Polite Conversations. 2017d. The Rightward Shift of Islam Critics. A Speech for BC Humanist Association. Available at: https://soundcloud.com/politeconversations/rightwardshift [Accessed 20 January 2021].

Polite Converstions. 2018. Lawrence Krauss: Allegations & Responses. Available at: https://soundcloud.com/politeconversations/krausspanel [Accessed 18 June 2021].

Polite Conversations. 2019a. The Christchurch Attack and Online Radicalization. Available at: https://soundcloud.com/politeconversations/christchurch [Accessed 20 January 2021].

Polite Conversations. 2019b. The IDW in Pakistan and Saudi Arabia. Available at: https://soundcloud.com/politeconversations/episode-58-the-idw-in-pakistan-saudi [Accessed 20 January 2021].

Polite Conversations. 2020. The Online World of Muslims. Available at: https://soundcloud.com/politeconversations/episode-59-the-online-world-of-muslims [Accessed 20 January 2021].

Polite Conversations. 2021. Cancel Culture. Available at: https://soundcloud.com/politeconversations/ep-62-cancel-culture [Accessed 5 March 2021].

Ramey, S. 2013. Creatio Ex Nihilo: Pew Forum and the "Nones". *Bulletin for the Study of Religion* [blog], January 25. Available at: https://bulletin.equinoxpub.com/2013/01/creatio-ex-nihilo-pew-forum-and-the-nones-2/ [Accessed 20 January 2021].

Rising. 2020. Zaid Jilani: Should Social Media Billionaires Be Held Personally Liable for Riots, Destruction. *YouTube*, August 31. Available at: www.youtube.com/watch?v=uiRfZYasaEM [Accessed 20 January 2021].

Rizvi, A. 2016. *The Atheist Muslim: A Journey from Religion to Reason.* New York: St. Martin's Press.

RT. 2013. (Non)Mass Movement: Atheist Mega Churches Take Western World by Storm. *RT*, November 11. Available at: www.rt.com/news/atheist-mega-churches-west-518/ [Accessed 20 January 2021].

Savage, L., Sloan, W. 2017. Religilous. *Michael and Us* [podcast], January 16. Available at: https://soundcloud.com/michael-and-us/episode-23-religulous [Accessed 20 January 2021].

Savage, L., Sloan, W. 2018. Expelled: No Intelligence Allowed. *Michael and Us* [podcast]. Available at: https://soundcloud.com/michael-and-us/53-expelled-no-intelligence-allowed [Accessed 20 January 2021].

Scheidt, H. 2021. *Practicing Atheism: Culture, Media, and Ritual in the Contemporary Atheist Network*. New York: Oxford University Press.

Seymour, R. 2013. *Unhitched: The Trial of Christopher Hitchens*. London: Verso.

Sheedy, M. 2017. Religious Are Intrinsically Violent. In: B. Stoddard, C. Martin, eds., *Stereotyping Religion: Critiquing Clichés*, pp. 23–40. London: Bloomsbury.

Stedman, C. 2012. *Faitheist: How an Atheist Found Common Ground with the Religious*. Boston: Beacon Press.

Stern, A. 2019. *Proud Boys and the White Ethnostate: How the Alt-Right Is Warping the American Imagination*. Boston, MA: Beacon Press.

Taibbi, M. 2019. *Hate Inc.: Why Today's Media Makes Us Despise One Another*. New York: OR Books.

Thiessen, J., Wilkins-Laflame, S. 2020. *None of the above: Having No Religion in the United States and Canada*. New York: New York University Press.

Tomlins, S., Bullivant, S. C., eds. 2016. *The Atheist Bus Campaign: Global Manifestations and Responses*. Leiden: Brill.

Vliek, M. 2018. Challenging Secularities, Challenging Religion: Secularist Ex-Muslims Voices in British Debate on Islam and Freedom of Expression. *Journal of Religion in Europe*, 11(4), pp. 348–377.

Vliek, M. 2019. "It's Not Just about Faith": Narratives of Transformation When Moving Out of Islam in the Netherlands and Britain. *Islam and Christian-Muslim Relations*, 30(3), pp. 1–22.

Warraq, I. 2003. *Leaving Islam: Apostates Speak Out*. Amherst: Prometheus Books.

Weiss, B. 2018. Meet the Renegades of the Intellectual Dark Web. *New York Times*, May 8. Available at: www.nytimes.com/2018/05/08/opinion/intellectual-dark-web.html [Accessed 20 January 2021].

Wikipedia. 2020. List of Former Muslims. Available at: https://en.wikipedia.org/wiki/List_of_former_Muslims [Accessed 20 January 2021].

Wikipedia. 2021a. List of Former Muslims. Available at: https://en.wikipedia.org/wiki/List_of_former_Muslims [Accessed 20 January 2021].

Wikipedia. 2021b. Regressive Left. Available at: https://en.wikipedia.org/wiki/Regressive_left [Accessed 20 January 2021].

Wikipedia. 2021c. The Satanic Temple. Available at: https://en.wikipedia.org/wiki/The_Satanic_Temple [Accessed 20 January 2021].

YouTube. 2011. Christopher Hitchens and Newt Gingrich: What Kind of War Are We Fighting? October 17. Available at: www.youtube.com/watch?v=OET1UGhJIYI [Accessed 20 January 2021].

Zuboff, S. 2019. *The Age of Surveillance Capitalism: The Fight for a Human Future at the New Frontier of Power*. London: Profile Books.

Conclusion

Throughout this book, I have considered how the secular has been re-imagined in the wake of ground-shaking political events such as the fall of the Soviet Union, the terrorist attacks of 9/11, and the election of Donald Trump. By focusing on how the secular is produced through conflict and through changes in communication, I have aimed to call attention to the political nature of this category, and how its uses are conditioned by changing structures of political and technological organization. When considering the allure of culture wars, the incentive structures of social media, and the boundless growth of online spaces, it strikes me that we have only just begun to map this ever-expanding digital secular terrain.

Following the unprecedented Indigenous-led Idle No More movement (2012–2013), and the partial adoption of the Truth and Reconciliation Commission's (2008–2015) ninety-four calls to action, Canada has seen a significant increase in Indigenous representation in media, popular culture, parliament, and in educational curricula. At the same time, there has been a growing revitalization of Indigenous epistemologies (or ways of knowing) within various communities, which is still in an early stage of development. In time, such trends may create different and competing models of governance and interaction that are currently unrecognizable within more mainstream 'secular' modes of deliberation.

I call attention to the Indigenous question in Canada here in conclusion to highlight an example of Asad's point about translation that opens this book, where he states, "it is quite another [thing] for the anthropologist to approach 'the native' with the possibility of learning something important for her own form of life that might help to transform how that life is understood" (2018: 9). After 500-plus years of colonization, including dispossession of land, forced assimilation through residential schools, and a host of other policies that attempted to assimilate Indigenous people into Euro-Christian forms of knowledge and governance, the changes that have been taking place over the last decade or so in Canada offer a unique lens into the state of the secular and the fragility of Western values. While there are many differences between Indigenous histories and, say, the many Muslim cultures that are growing in Euro-Western states like Canada, one line of comparison that tracks the flows of the secular in both cases is the relative power of these communities and what that means for the type of force they might exert on conceptions of Western identity. Whereas Muslims are seen as newcomers that are expected to assimilate into a broader Canadian multiculturalism, Indigenous communities can make a claim to being the original inhabitants of the land and have leveraged that status in ways that are slowly changing how younger generations, in particular, relate to conceptions of knowledge, history, identity, and modes of social interaction. Paying attention to these changing configurations of knowledge and power provides yet another window into how Western identities and subjectivities are being reshaped, and the coordinates of the secular along with it.

Work cited

Asad, T. 2018. *Secular Translations: Nation-State, Modern Self, and Calculative Reason.* New York: Columbia University Press.

Index

For Product Safety Concerns and Information please contact our EU representative GPSR@taylorandfrancis.com
Taylor & Francis Verlag GmbH, Kaufingerstraße 24, 80331 München, Germany

www.ingramcontent.com/pod-product-compliance
Lightning Source LLC
LaVergne TN
LVHW010932110826
845149LV00013B/2565

* 9 7 8 1 0 3 2 0 8 0 1 6 1 *